"The world cannot hear what the church is saying beca[...] get in the way. Discipleship and character formation a[...] Christians to embrace a way of life that lines up with the words of the gospel which we proclaim. If we allow this book to seep into our souls, the mission of God will be advanced in our world."

—M. Scott Boren, consultant and author of *Missional Small Groups*

"What has become a trend of late in moral thought has been true of Christians for centuries—character counts! Much more than virtue alone, good character in the Scriptures has always been about right action. Joyfully, Blackaby and Wilkes provide readers with a holistic view of Christian character through the hearts and hands of the great saints in the Bible. They deliver us an invitation to learn from our Bible heroes and live changed lives as a result."

—Larry C. Ashlock, DMin, PhD, professor of pastoral leadership and ethics, director of the *Doctor of Ministry Program, B. H. Carroll Theological Institute*

"Blackaby and Wilkes have done it again! This thoughtful, practical, and challenging book is a leadership must-read! Your heart will be touched and enlightened by the stories, encouraged by the devotional helps, and developed by the study resources provided. As you journey along with the characters of the biblical narrative, you will learn from their example; the good, the bad, the positive, the negative, the right, and the wrong. Your own journey will be impacted as you grow in character and closer to the heart of God, better equipped to impact your world wherever He leads."

—Debra L. Brown, president and CEO, Brown Governance Inc.

"This wonderful book by Dr. Norman Blackaby and Pastor Gene Wilkes addresses a personal quality that is unfortunately lacking among so many of today's leaders—character. However, it is a quality that God is most concerned to cultivate in His people. I have known Dr. Blackaby for the last 5 years as one of our Dallas Baptist University professors and Dr. Wilkes for more than 40 years as a friend. Both men are of great character and integrity. As the authors emphasize, godly character goes much deeper than even outward morality and is a genuine integrity of the heart flowing from a humble, intimate, and abiding fellowship with God. With rich lessons drawn from both good and bad examples in the Scriptures, this book encourages us all to reflect on how God uses conflicts, hardships, and even failures to test and develop the character of Christ in us for His glory and purpose."

—Gary Cook, president, Dallas Baptist University

"I think that most of us who name the name of Christ believe that character is important, even key. But what makes up Christian character? How can you build it? Is who we are in Christ really more important than what we do for Christ? In *Character: The Pulse of a Disciple's Heart,* Blackaby and Wilkes explore God's view of Christian character, focusing on leaders from Scripture, and building a biblical model for a Christian character standard. For any Christian seeking to serve God in the most effective means possible, this book is a great help and a must-read."

—Dr. John B. Sorensen, president, Evangelism Explosion International

New Hope® Publishers
P. O. Box 12065
Birmingham, AL 35202-2065
newhopedigital.com
New Hope Publishers is a division of WMU®.

Library of Congress Cataloging-in-Publication Data

Blackaby, Norman C.
 Character : the pulse of a disciple's heart / Norman Blackaby and Gene Wilkes.
   p. cm.
 ISBN 978-1-59669-347-0 (sc)
 1. Character--Religious aspects--Christianity. 2. Character--Biblical teaching. I. Wilkes, C. Gene. II. Title.
 BV4599.5.C45B53 2012
 248.4--dc23
                              2012007250

ISBN-10: 1-59669-347-9
ISBN-13: 978-1-59669-347-0
N124101 • 0512 • 4M1

Cover & interior design: Michel Lê

CHARACTER
THE PULSE OF A DISCIPLE'S HEART

NORMAN BLACKABY
GENE WILKES

NEW HOPE
PUBLISHERS

Birmingham, Alabama

To Kim, my wife, and a living example of character we write about here, and to Legacy Church who God has used to mold my character.

GENE WILKES

I dedicate this book to my wife, Dana, who has faithfully allowed God to shape her character beginning as a fifth-grade young lady until the present.

NORMAN BLACKABY

CONTENTS

How God Develops Character

Acknowledgments

A book about character requires people of character who are behind it. We would not have a message or the urgency to share it without the person and leader of Jesus, who is our example of godlike character. Christlike character is the standard for all measures of character, and we are humbled to have been called by Him to be His servants where He has placed us. We are grateful to our wives who encourage us and support us in projects like this one. Dana Blackaby has read and reread the manuscript throughout the writing and editing process, and her careful work is invaluable to what you read here. We want to thank Andrea Mullins of New Hope Publishers who invited us to write this book, and Joyce Dinkins and the team at New Hope who produced the book you hold in your hand. Writers are helpless without editors and production teams. The team members at New Hope are true servants of the Lord. We also want to thank Dr. Gary Cook and Dallas Baptist University for the opportunity to lead the PhD seminar in biblical servant leadership that was the seedbed for this topic and project. Gene thanks the people of Legacy Church who consider his writing ministry part of his ministry to them and to the big C church as well. Gene also thanks Legacy's staff and leadership team who exhibit character and work at the highest levels to carry out the mission and vision of Legacy which allows Gene the freedom to write.

INTRODUCTION

A Little Bit of Background

S everal years ago I (Norman) was asked to co-teach a seminar on Biblical Servant Leadership with Dr. Gene Wilkes for a university PhD program. I did not know Gene at the time, but was aware of his writing and speaking related to Christian leadership. Gene and I had very different backgrounds and ministry experiences. His field of study is in New Testament and mine is in biblical backgrounds and Old Testament. I wondered how we would approach the seminar and whether our teaching styles would be complementary. From the very first semester, we found a common ground: a deep love of God and His Word, which is the basis for our lives and ministry. We have continued to teach together over the years, and it is a joy each time I have the privilege of working with Gene.

While we continue to teach together, both of us remain very active in the local church setting. Gene continues to serve as the senior pastor of a church he has led for more than 20 years. While I teach full-time in a university setting, I continue to serve in my local church, as well as speak in churches and conferences when time permits. God has also placed on both of our hearts a deep burden for missions that places us in a variety of unique ministry settings around the globe.

God has placed us in diverse ministries, from the local church and mission field settings, to the seminary and university classroom. Regardless of where we serve, we encounter one common issue that rises to the forefront: the issue of *character*.

Whether we are teaching a singles Sunday School class, counseling church members, leading conferences, or teaching PhD seminars, we find people wrestling with issues related to character. First, we see in many people a deep desire to develop godly character in their own lives. Further, we encounter Christians who need help relating to people who seem to have a lack of character.

Our initial thought for this project was to create a helpful tool to assist our teaching endeavors. However, as we moved farther into the project, it became clear that we did not want this work to be limited to a classroom setting; rather, we want this work used to encourage and guide people wrestling through issues of life in real-world settings. While we hope that our students will enjoy this book, it is truly our desire that this offering be a blessing to those in the church who desire to walk closely with our Lord in the challenging times in which we live.

CHAPTER 1

The Importance of Character

haracter is a matter that has been pushed to the forefront of our society with great intensity in recent years. All too often, issues of character are highlighted by moral failure. The news media quickly pounce upon a story of a famous politician, sports figure, or church leader caught in a career-ending scandal. On a more local level, there are stories of those in the community who have "fallen short" in various areas and now have to pick up the pieces of their lives which have been ruined by a deep-rooted character flaw. In many of these instances there is an outcry for character or the recognition of its importance, but little is offered as a solution for this call. At the same time that the world is highlighting the failure of so many, there are countless others who have determined to allow God to develop their character in such a way that their lives are making significant contributions in all walks of life. What determines if a person will live out God's full potential for his or her life? We believe it is the issue of character. Character is the single most distinguishing aspect of a person's life. No matter one's training, traits, or skills, character determines who a person is and how he or she will respond in critical issues of life. God cares more about our character than our skills, personality, or intelligence because biblically, character is a matter of the "heart." The Bible provides numerous examples and teachings related to one's heart. God chose people whom He could mold through their circumstances, so that He could use them for His eternal purposes.

Character Is a Matter of the Heart

CHAPTER 2

D epending on the setting, the term *character* can have different meanings. Character can have positive as well as negative implications; we all know that person who can be described as "quite a character." However, most of the time, character refers to positive attributes in a person. But character is more than simply positive attributes. We can admire a person who never gives up in the face of difficulties. We can watch from a distance or work alongside a person who is always determined to get the job done and admire this quality in the person, but this attribute may or may not reflect godly character. Certainly the desire to complete or finish responsibilities is admirable; but if you look below the surface, it may simply be an expression of a very stubborn or prideful person whose vanity will not allow for failure. For Christians, character is not simply an assessment of our admirable qualities, but something that goes beyond ourselves. Biblically, character is defined by the quality of our intimate fellowship with God. In our relationship with God, we find our moral compass, calling, and spiritual strength to live in an intimate relationship with Him and to complete what God has called us to do.

The Bible describes this intimate relationship between a person and God as residing in the heart. In the Old Testament this takes the form of God calling His people to:

• love Him with all your heart (Deuteronomy 6:5);

• to seek Him with all your heart (Deuteronomy 4:29);

• to incline your heart unto Him (Joshua 24:23);

• to walk before Him with all your heart (2 Chronicles 6:14);

• and to have willing hearts that bring offerings to the Lord (Exodus 35:5). We could go on and on regarding Scriptures describing this relationship as a matter of the heart. The heart was used to describe the condition of persons' relationship with God—it was simply a matter of the heart. Those who did not honor or walk with God in obedience were described as "hard of heart" in the New Testament (Mark 3:5), and even Christ's own disciples were rebuked for their unbelief, described as "hardness of heart" (Mark 16:14). When God spoke through the prophets, calling the people to repent, it was in terms of the heart, as God promised to take away their stony heart and give them a heart of flesh (Ezekiel 11:19; 36:26). Probably the most encouraging reference to people's relationship with God in the Old Testament is God's promise of a New Covenant (speaking of the relationship that would be established through Christ) in the Book of Jeremiah. It is here, in chapter 31, when the prophet claims that in this new relationship God would write His law on the human heart (v. 33). In the New Testament, we see this occurring as the Spirit of Christ dwells in our hearts in Ephesians 3:17, or the love of God dwelling in our hearts through the Spirit (in Romans 5:5).

Jesus seldom described Himself to others, but on one occasion, as He offered rest and healing to those who came to Him, He acknowledged He was "gentle and humble in heart" (Matthew 11:29). This description of His heart was counter to how He described our hearts. When confronted by the religious leaders about His disciples' disrespect for their religious traditions, Jesus explained that what goes into a person physically is not what defiles a person, but "what comes out of the mouth proceeds from the heart, and this defiles a person" (Matthew 15:18 ESV). The single, overarching commandment of God for all who trust Him is to "love the Lord your God with all your heart and with all your soul and with all your mind" (Matthew 22:37; also see Deuteronomy 6:5).

Another side of this "heart relationship" is that God desires for us to know His heart as well. When God was looking for someone to serve Him as He directed the children of Israel, He describes the character He desires with these words: "I will raise up for myself a faithful priest who shall do according to what is in my heart and mind" (1 Samuel 2:35). God was going to raise up a person to do what was on His heart, and we see this happen through the life of Samuel. The New Testament tells us that God's people will know what is on His heart through the Holy Spirit who will reveal the "deep things of God" (1 Corinthians 2:6-16).

Character is a matter of the heart: it is the quality of the believer's intimate fellowship with God. It is expressed in a multitude of ways as we seek to honor God in our daily lives. It is what determines how we respond in times of crisis or how quickly we obey the direction of God with an open and glad attitude. Character is an ongoing process of relating to our Lord, walking with Him and honoring Him in our daily lives.

CHAPTER 3

The Need for a
Biblical Approach
and Why We Chose
Case Studies

T here are many different approaches to writing a book on character. It is tempting simply to provide a how-to book based on our years of study and experiences in ministry. We could outline the marks of Christian character and provide a plan of study for each of these attributes as well as recommend follow-up sources. While this approach can be helpful, we have a deep conviction that Christians need to learn to "dig" into the Scripture and, as much as possible, see what the Scripture teaches on character. There is just something about allowing the Holy Spirit to guide a person as he or she opens the Bible (or scrolls through the text) that every Christ follower must learn. While we will share our insights into the passage and make specific application of the passages, our desire is that you learn to depend primarily on the Scriptures.

The approach we have chosen for our study is to look at the narrative passages in the Bible. There are certainly other important teachings on character, but the narrative passages give us a glimpse into the lives of the people in the Bible. We see them as they wrestled with the good and bad circumstances of life, as they dealt with successes and failures, and as they sought to understand God's will and His plan. The most exciting part of this process is seeing how God walked with people during each circumstance. Often narrative passages of Scripture do not explain the text or the truths that are imbedded into the story. When reading narrative Scripture, there is an understanding that the reader is expected to work through the text and make decisions on the lives and actions of the characters in the story. The reader needs to evaluate the circumstances surrounding the character and press their actions against the truths of God.

During this process you will find at times that the people studied reveal amazing character and set high examples for anyone desiring to honor God. At other times, the biblical figures fall short of honoring God and their story will serve as a warning or challenge to your own life. As in any good story, the narrative passages will engage you in a way that you will identify with the characters and circumstances. They will force you to evaluate your own life against their examples, whether negative or positive. In this process, we have addressed some familiar examples as well as some examples that you may not have studied before. Some of the accounts tell the story of some of the Bible's greatest figures, while others may look at someone whose name is not even given in the passage. However, each person recorded in the Scriptures was placed there for a specific reason to help us understand our God, His purposes, and how we can seek to worship and honor Him in greater ways.

Reading the Cases

Each biblical story is introduced with a description of the particular focus we are going to study. However, we may simply address one of the people in the account or zero in on one particular issue while the text may have several key issues. It is our hope that these chapters will foster or encourage you to expand your study of the people described. To this end, we have provided suggestions for further study at the end of each case study. You may find these suggestions for further study personally helpful in your regular devotional times, or as talking points should you wish to use this book in a Sunday School class, Bible study group, or in an accountability setting.

A Challenge to Read the Scriptures

We encourage you to thoroughly read the Scriptures that are listed at the front of each chapter. We will go over the verses in the chapters to draw out specific truths and apply them to our lives. However, you will shortchange your study to simply jump over the suggested Scripture readings to our comments. We challenge you to work through the study with us so that you can make this a practice in your own devotional life (remember that we will be providing additional study at the end of each chapter).

A Division of Cases

We have divided the case studies into two sections. The first group of studies looks at the process through which character was developed or revealed in the individual. At times the Scripture explains the process of character development in great detail, while at other times a person's character is simply stated or implied from the circumstances. Many of the studies in the first section, "How God Develops Character," could have been placed in the second section, Character That Makes a Difference. However, in these cases the heart of the passage presented examples of the process more than the effect of character. The second section includes studies that reveal how God was able to use a person for His kingdom because of the character they exhibited. In this section we can see how certain people, who strived to have godly character, were used to impact other people. While several of the studies could fit in either category, it is our hope that as you work through these divisions, you will be challenged not only to strive to be a person of godly character, but to have such a strong relationship with God that He will be able to use you to make a radical difference in the lives of those around you.

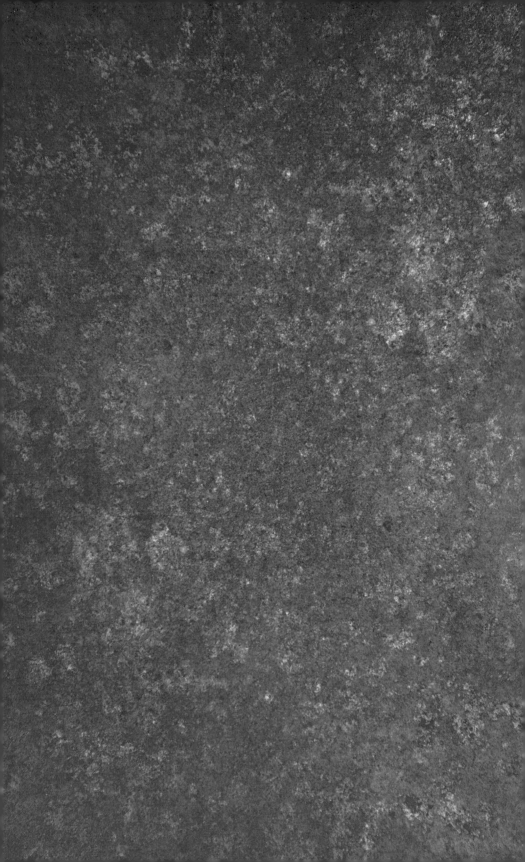

HOW GOD DEVELOPS CHARACTER

CHAPTER 4

Moses: Growing in Humility

The Bible describes Moses as "a very humble man, more humble than anyone else on the face of the earth" (Numbers 12:3). We don't find that description about another human in the rest of the Bible. But, Moses was not always a humble man. He committed a crime of passion, then ran and hid in the desert, and relentlessly questioned God when God called him to free Israel from Egypt. If Moses did not always display humility, how did God mold the character of this leader the Bible calls the most humble man on the face of the earth?

Jesus Is Our Standard

Before we examine the event that revealed Moses' humble character, we must see what the Bible says about humility in the character of Jesus, the One by whom all others are measured.

Jesus described himself as "gentle and humble in heart" (Matthew 11:29). The word for *gentle* can also be translated *humble*, and it is the same Greek word used to describe Moses in the Greek translation of the Old Testament. *Humble* in the New Testament verse is a synonym of gentle and means one who is lowly of heart. Jesus taught humility was a kingdom virtue when He said to His disciples, "For all those who exalt themselves will be humbled, and those who humble themselves will be exalted" (Luke 14:11). Jesus did not simply teach about humility as a virtue, he practiced it. When the Holy Spirit inspired Paul to reflect on the life of Jesus, as an example of how our attitudes should be toward one another, he wrote, "And being found in the appearance as a man, he humbled himself by becoming obedient to death—even death on a cross!" (Philippians 2:8). Jesus humbled all He was to the will of the Father, which included death on a cross. Biblical humility is submitting to the plans of God over your own plans. It is trusting God to the point that if He guides you to lay down your life for another, you will do that.

Humility is knowing who you are before Holy God and submitting all you are to His leadership in your life through His Word and Spirit. Peter, writing to the early church and following Jesus' lead, exhorted Christians: "Humble yourselves, therefore, under God's mighty hand, that he may lift you up in due time" (1 Peter 5:6). Humility is not a false emotion of weakness but the heart-guided choice to take your place under the leadership of God and to be obedient to His revealed plans for your life.

A Defining Moment

To interpret the Bible correctly we must always observe what is happening on either side of the passage we study. We are tempted to choose a single phrase or verse if it seems to support our preconceived understanding of God or reality. Our goal, however, should be to *allow the Bible to read us, rather than for us to read it.*

Read Numbers 12 to learn the full story around the statement that revealed the superlative nature of Moses' humility.

The context of the statement about Moses' character was a challenge by Miriam and Aaron to Moses' leadership of Israel after they left Egypt. The people had complained (again) that the pastry-like *manna* God provided for food in the desert was no longer to their liking, and they wanted meat (Numbers 11:4-6). After the Lord empowered the elders of the camp with the Spirit, He sent a wind that "drove quail in from the sea. It scattered them up to two cubits [about 3 feet] deep all around the camp, as far as a day's walk in any direction" (11:31). The people asked for meat, and the Lord gave them meat! They ate it greedily and some became sick from eating the quail because the Bible says they "had craved other food" (11:34). This spirit of discontent among the people may have influenced the two leaders who challenged Moses. A negative attitude is like a flu virus. Those who come in contact with it most often catch it.

A Sibling Challenge

Both Aaron and Miriam played important leadership roles in Israel. They both loved the Lord as evidenced by their service and praise to Him. God appointed Aaron to speak for Moses before Pharaoh, which led to the deliverance of Israel (Exodus 4:16). Moses gave his brother the priestly responsibility of building and maintaining the Tabernacle (Exodus 28:1). He was Israel's first high priest. A fault in Aaron's character was revealed while Moses was on the mountain receiving the commandments from the Lord. In the absence of God's chosen leader, the high priest of Yahweh allowed the people to build a golden calf that they could worship (Exodus 32:1–6). Although Moses interceded with God for the sins of the people, he chastised Aaron and God disciplined the people (32:7–35).

Miriam was the sister of both Moses and Aaron. She protected her little brother Moses when Pharaoh's daughter found him as a baby floating in the Nile. She risked her life when she offered to provide a nurse for the infant, but the daughter of Pharaoh accepted her offer, and Moses was raised as Egyptian royalty (Exodus 2:1–10). The Bible described Miriam as a "prophetess" who led others in singing and dancing before the Lord after the Red Sea closed on the pursuing army of Egypt (Exodus 15:20-21). She was also privy to her brothers' conversations with the God of Israel because of her close association with Moses and Aaron.

Aaron, the high priest, and Miriam, the prophetess, decided they could lead as well as Moses. Their reason to disqualify Moses as leader was that he had married a Cushite, a non-Israelite (Numbers 12:1). Some commentators equate Cush with Midian, the land of Moses' wife, Zipporah (Exodus 2:21). But this complaint was a smokescreen for the real issue behind their challenge. Moses married Zipporah before the Exodus, and if this were the real problem, they could have brought it up at an earlier time (Exodus 2:21). They asked themselves, "Has the Lord spoken only through Moses . . . Hasn't he also spoken through us?" (Numbers 12:2). Pride, not a technical issue about the ethnicity of Moses' wife, drove them to challenge God's chosen leader. They believed they could speak for the Lord as well as their brother.

Pride is the opposite of humility. Power—yes, even spiritual power—can puff people up to think they can lead as well as the one the Lord has set over them. We may argue that pressure, stress, or adversity reveals the true character of someone, but power can also expose one's character. Nitin Nohria, dean of the Harvard Business School, observed in a newspaper interview that Abraham Lincoln said people think the real test of a person's character is how they deal with adversity, but a much better test of a person's character is how they deal with power. I've been more often disappointed with how the character of people is revealed when they've been given power.

Aaron and Miriam were given positional power to lead among the people of God. That power exposed their prideful character, which motivated them to consider themselves worthy of Moses' place of leadership.

Moses, based on the Bible's description of his character, might have let the challenge go, but Numbers 12:2 says, "And the Lord heard this." The next verse is the parenthetical statement that breaks the action of the story. The challenge to Aaron and Miriam's insurrection came from the Lord, not Moses. This tells us something about the character of both of them.

What Does True Humility Look Like?

When the Lord heard Miriam's and Aaron's rebellious hearts, He called all three siblings out to the tent of meeting (Numbers 12:4). He summoned Aaron and Miriam forward, and when they stood in His presence, the Lord basically told them, "If I want to reveal myself among the people, there are prophets I have chosen for that purpose. As for Moses, of whom you think you can speak for Me as well as he can, he is My chosen and faithful servant. I speak to him 'face to face' and not in riddles. So, then why did you not fear speaking against this one I have chosen?" (my paraphrase of vv. 6–8). The Lord made it clear the two siblings had no right or standing to challenge the one God had chosen to lead His people. They should fear, not challenge, God's servant leader.

When the Lord's presence left the tent, Miriam had leprous skin, a most dreaded disease among the people for it meant separation from her tribe and nation as well as living in agonizing pain. She could no longer serve the Lord and would be forced to live outside the camp in this condition (Leviticus 13). When Aaron saw this, he begged forgiveness from his brother. Aaron saw himself from God's perspective and rightfully called what they had done "the sin we have so foolishly committed" (Numbers 12:11). Rather than allow his sister's condition to stand, Moses cried out to the Lord, "Please, God, heal her!" The Lord healed her but required she remain outside the camp for seven days as if she had been disgraced by her father (v. 14). After seven days she was healed and returned to the camp and to her place of leadership.

Why would Moses not allow his brother and sister to suffer the consequences of their sin? Why didn't he allow the "anger of the Lord" to burn against them longer? The answer lies in the biblical statement about his humility. Moses interceded for his rebellious sister because he knew the position he led from was not of his doing. The Lord affirmed this reality when he spoke to the two coup-attempting siblings. God called him and empowered him to lead, and his humble heart was the foundation of his security. It was not his efforts that won him a place at the top of Israel's leadership. Moses depended upon the Lord for his position, power, and insight to lead. Humility is dependence upon God to provide and sustain you. If you are a leader, it is the certainty from which you can pray even for those who try to take your job.

Moses displayed his humble heart when he interceded for those who questioned his position of leadership. Pride would not have allowed such a gracious act. How do we overcome pride and gain the strength to serve others? Moses' humility was built upon his devout dependence upon the Lord. He had not sought his position of leadership; nor had he fought to keep it. He depended on the One who had called him and proclaimed him the leader of Israel for his confidence to lead. He was humble because he trusted the Lord for all he had and did. This is true humility.

God developed Moses' character through the selfish motives of his brother and sister. His character was revealed when he prayed even for those who had tried to bring him down. God tests our character by allowing others to challenge us and to strive against us. These times of challenge demand a humility that is founded on our deep dependence upon God and trust that our position of leadership—whatever that may be—is the result of His guidance and grace in our lives, not our hard work and intelligence.

To trust God for where and whom you lead and to submit to His will and ways is the seedbed for humility. Otherwise, you will become prideful of your perceived accomplishments, and you will feel the need to protect what you have gained and to ward off those who may want what you have. Solomon observed people who labored without trust in God, and he concluded, "What do people get for all the toil and anxious striving with which they labor under the sun? All their days their work is grief and pain; even at night their minds do not rest. This too is meaningless" (Ecclesiastes 2:22–23).

Without biblical humility, which is founded on total dependence upon the Lord, we are left to a life of "anxious striving" against others so that "even at night [our] minds do not rest." Depend on the Lord daily for all you have, and you will find a humility that will serve you as you live out God's call on your life.

A Challenge for Our Day

- Make a list of people and places God has given you to lead. These may include your home, school, neighborhood, church or office. How would you describe your trust in God for the place and people you lead?
- Are there people in your life who challenge you about your decisions or the direction in which you want to lead them? If so, write their names on a piece of paper and an emotion you feel toward them next to their names.

Why do you feel that way toward them? Do they expose your pride, which leads to your emotion? Are their challenges legitimate?

• Spend time in prayer confessing your dependence upon God for all you are and have and take time to pray for those who challenge you. Ask God to reveal His purpose in each of these relationships so you may experience true humility.

Further Study

Take time to dig a little deeper into the life of Moses to learn more about how God molded his character and used his life to help others trust Him.

• Find articles on Moses, Aaron, and Miriam in a Bible dictionary or encyclopedia. Or, look up the passages in the texts above to learn more about who they were in the plan of God.

• Reread Numbers 12 again. As you do, put yourself in Moses' place. How would you respond? Would verse 3 describe you? Also, put yourself in Miriam's or Aaron's place. Have you ever felt this way toward another leader? How did that turn out?

• Read Numbers 11, 12, and 13 to discover a larger context for the challenge of Miriam and Aaron to Moses' leadership.

CHAPTER 5

Joshua: Character in the Midst of Failure

ave you ever heard the saying "You don't fall from the valley, but from the mountaintop"? While we can obviously find exceptions to this adage, the meaning is that we had better be careful and not let our guard down when we think everything is going well. It is often after times of great victory or a recommitment of our lives to God that we experience our greatest struggles or failures. If any of you have ever worked with young people, you probably have witnessed the emotional and spiritual high they experience during and immediately following a summer camp or mission trip. There are often times where the young people come before the church and share all that God did in their lives during a retreat or missions trip. There are declarations of fresh commitments before the church but, often shortly after the event, the struggles of life press in and many of these bold declarations for God fall to the wayside. As we get older there is a tendency to make less bold or public commitments. It is not, however, that we have less of these spiritual highs as we get older. Rather, we come to realize how difficult it is to maintain new commitments, and we are not as quick to declare them publicly.

We know that during this lifetime, we are going to struggle and make mistakes in the Christian life. We often quote verses such as: "If we say we have no sin, we deceive ourselves, and the truth is not in us. If we confess our sins, he is faithful and just to forgive us our sins and to cleanse us from all unrighteousness" (1 John 1:8-9 ESV). That we are going to sin is a given. How we deal with our failures is a matter of character, and this character will most often be the determining factor in how God can use us after a time of failure.

When we think about the heroes of the Old Testament, we see men and women who showed amazing faith and dedication, often revealed during times of sin and failure. Joshua, the son of Nun, is one of these heroes of the faith. His life provides a helpful example of the old saying "you often fall from a high point." In Joshua 9, the Scriptures record a glaring mistake on Joshua's part as he led the people of Israel in their occupation of the Promised Land. However, in the face of his failure he displays character that serves as a warning and an encouragement for those in Christian leadership. The mistake he makes is clearly of his own doing, but his quick recovery and restoration to the purposes of God provide a helpful example. Rather than becoming paralyzed in his mistake, or blaming others for his failure, he accepted the mistake, owned up to his responsibility, followed God, and was immediately brought back into the activity of God.

A Closer Look at the Text

Joshua 9 records events of the Israelite central campaign to take possession of the Promised Land. Under God's guidance they had taken the city of Jericho in Joshua 6. However, Israel experienced a stunning defeat at the city of Ai due to the sin of Achan and his family (Joshua 7:1–9). Once it was clear that Israel's defeat was due to the sin of Achan, Joshua dealt with the problem and, under God's direction attacked Ai again, this time defeating the Canaanite city-state (Joshua 7:10 to 8:29). The last portion of Joshua 8 has particular importance for our study. Following the victory, Joshua built an altar and offered sacrifices to the Lord, read all of the words of Moses to the people, and led them in a renewal of the Covenant (8:30–35). Heading into Joshua 9 we would expect to read of great victories as they have been reminded of the Law and are newly committed to serve God. However, what we see is far from what would be expected. Rather than Joshua leading the people to follow God in taking the rest of the land, he fails to seek after God and is tricked into making a covenant with the Gibeonite people. The mistake is worsened by the fact that Joshua and his leadership bound the entire Israelite people to this covenant. More importantly, the covenant was a blatant violation of God's command for Israel concerning the people of Palestine (Deuteronomy 20:16–18).

READ JOSHUA 9:1–27.

The Quick Decision

When you read a passage like this, it is easy to focus on the deceit of the Gibeonites. After all, they went to great lengths to fool Joshua and the other leaders of Israel. While not excusing them from their sin, we should remember their options were not very promising. They could have fled their homeland or been destroyed by Joshua and his army. We have to admit they certainly were creative in their self-preservation. However, the story is not about the Gibeonites; rather its focus is on the Israelites and, more specifically, Joshua and his leadership. How could he come from such an example of God's correction in dealing with Achan, as well as a renewal of the covenant, and make such a mistake? Let's look a little bit into Joshua and his decision.

Reading the text, it becomes clear that Joshua should have known better than to bind himself to this covenant. An immediate clue for Joshua was that the Gibeonites claimed to be from such a faraway country (v. 6), and they repeated that it was very far away in verse 9. There really was no need to make this covenant with a people located outside the Promised Land. Israel had been given the land of Canaan and was instructed to destroy the local Canaanite peoples of the land they were to occupy. Why would these foreign people be so anxious to make the covenant? There was no immediate threat from Israel. Did you catch how much pressure they put on Joshua to make this covenant? The text certainly doesn't record any "small talk" or much in the way of introductions in verse 6. When asked for more proof of their identity, the Gibeonites don't provide much information before pressing again for a covenant of peace in verse 11.

A second indication that Joshua should have slowed down this process was that the men of Israel called the Gibeonites "Hivites." Again, the Hivites were one of the people groups that Israel had been instructed to destroy when they entered the land (Deuteronomy 20:17). So, what was going on with Joshua? Why would he make such a hasty commitment in light of some glaring details that should have caused him alarm? Two aspects of his bad decision quickly arise. The first one is addressed in Joshua 9:14 when it states they "did not inquire of the Lord." Before we address this obvious issue, let's look at a couple preceding verses that shed light on this statement.

The Gibeonites were creative in their deception by using moldy bread and worn-out clothing, but the key to their deception is really found in their appeal to Joshua's pride in verses 9–10. "Because of the fame of the Lord your God. For we have heard . . ." How do you get a person to make a quick decision without really working through the issues or the ramifications of that decision? Appeal to his or her pride. Your God's reputation and His great victories are known abroad. We know who you are and how powerful you are. We know of your victories and you cause us to tremble, so we have traveled all this way. You people are famous! Influenced by flattery, Joshua makes a huge and obvious mistake. Verse 14 simply states they did not consult the Lord. Now this is the same group of leaders who witnessed the battle of Jericho and the way God denied their success as well as their victory at the city of Ai. This was the group that had just had a time of renewal and recommitment to God in which they had renewed the covenant (8:30-35). In fact, the text goes to great lengths to let the reader know that "there was not a word of all that Moses had commanded which Joshua did not read before the whole assembly of Israel" (8:35). Surely that reading and renewal of the Covenant would have emphasized the importance of consulting God!

If we are honest with ourselves, we can probably quickly identify with Joshua: "falling from a high point," a time of victory followed by a recommitment to honor and serve the Lord. The next event recorded is an act of disobedience. It is at this point of failure that we see the character of Joshua, which makes him stand out as a man of God. Three days after the covenant was made Joshua discovers that he has been tricked (9:16). Not only has he realized the mistake, but his own people "grumbled against the leaders" (9:18). In Hebrew it was the same verb used to describe how the children of Israel had grumbled against God in the wilderness.

It is interesting that even after they realized that they had been deceived, they do not attempt to get out of the agreement. After all, they had gone into this covenant in good faith and been tricked. However, this agreement and the swearing of the oath that had occurred in verse 15 had been sealed in an oath by the Lord God of Israel. If they forsook their oath, they would experience the wrath of Yahweh (9:20). Joshua can't go back on his agreement. However, he does make the Gibeonites slaves, woodcutters, and water carriers for the house of God because of their lies and deceit (9:23).

Character Revealed: Staying the Course in the Face of a Mistake

This account of Joshua is important because it reveals his character in the midst of failure. In particular, this was not failure from a defeat or bad luck, but due to his choices. Let's look at several key truths coming from the passage. Did you notice a difference in Joshua that appears to be lacking in leadership of our day? We don't see Joshua attempting to put the blame on the Gibeonites for his failure. They clearly deceived him and he admonished them (9:22–23), but it was his choice and lack of consulting God that caused him to make such a foolish mistake. The signs were all there for Joshua, but he chose not to see them. He was not forced to make a covenant of peace with these people in violation of God's commands, and there was no excuse offered except an admission of the mistake and a call to act honorably despite their unwise commitment.

Joshua was not alone in this poor decision; the rulers and leaders of Israel were "co-conspirators" in this decision. Their involvement was evident as the people voiced their complaints not simply at Joshua, but also at the "leaders." Again, in our day it seems that the quick and easy response of leadership is often to place the blame on someone else, to find a "scapegoat" for the wrong. There is no indication that Joshua or the other leaders attempted to blame each other. They all assumed responsibility, and Joshua made the best out of the deal with the Gibeonites. Accepting their responsibility and consequences freed Joshua to move from his blunder to continue leading the people in God's mission of taking the land (Joshua 10).

Now, how would you respond to a complaining crowd of people? In this case they had a legitimate complaint against the leadership. It almost seems like the tables have been turned here: Joshua had botched it, and the people were angered at his sin. It would have been an easy choice, in light of the complaining, simply to void this covenant in light of the deceit and the people's attitude toward the Gibeonites. But, unlike his first decision, he does think of the Lord. "We have given them our oath by the Lord, the God of Israel, and we cannot touch them now" (9:19). Joshua and the other leaders stood for what was right and honorable, even if it was going to cost them to do so. Rather than falter in the face of legitimate complaints, they honored God by honoring their commitment. It is as if he is stating, yes, we messed up here, but we are not going to do it again by failing to keep our word. If we look ahead to chapter 10, Israel will have to enter into a war with the Canaanites in order to defend the Gibeonites.

The Impact of Character

GOD USES PEOPLE WHO ACCEPT RESPONSIBILITY FOR THEIR MISTAKES. Joshua's quick decision and pride allowed him to be taken advantage of and fooled into disobeying God's command. Rather than compound the mistake by placing the blame on others or making excuses, he and the Israelite leadership simply state: "we made the agreement and now we are going to stick with it." The fact that Joshua had not consulted the Lord in the decision did not change the mission or plans of God for Israel to occupy the land. Joshua's poor judgment had not changed the fact that he was expected to lead the people in this endeavor. Rather than wasting time in a "blame game," his heart was to get back on track as quickly as possible. It is this character on display that fosters the unity where all the leadership go before the people to explain how they are going to keep their word to God.

Following this event, Joshua confronts the Gibeonites and makes them servants of Israel. Accepting responsibility for the failure safeguarded the leadership from division; the text reveals a unity among the leadership as well as the affirmation of Joshua's key role.

GOD HONORS PEOPLE WHO KEEP HIS WORD EVEN WHEN IT IS UNPOPULAR AND POSSIBLY COSTLY. Opposition is a common occurrence in the life of a Christian leader. The most courageous and godly leaders will face "grumblings" toward their leadership. Joshua and his leadership were in the wrong when they made this covenant. However, in the face of being deceived by one group and facing complaints from their own people, Joshua displays character when he honors his word, the covenant, and in turn, the God he served. Character demands that our integrity, as well as the reputation of the One we serve, is not quickly dismissed or pushed aside because we feel the circumstances are unfair or difficult. In light of the pressure from his own people, he could have simply taken the easy road and justified not keeping his word. While this would have been easy and most likely easily justified, it would have put the children of Israel in jeopardy with God and His purposes. If we look into the next chapter, we see how committed Joshua was to keeping his word in that he takes his army to protect the Gibeonites from the surrounding kings. Joshua was not simply committed in word, but he put his army in jeopardy to honor his end of the covenant. God intervened and provided an amazing victory on Joshua's behalf. Clearly Joshua's character in keeping his word is recognized and honored by God when He causes the sun to stand still to provide the Israelites a victory over the Canaanites.

GOD RESTORES AND USES PEOPLE WHO DO NOT GIVE UP IN THE MIDST OF PERSONAL FAILURE. Personal failure can quickly sideline us from serving God and leading his people. However, it is God who must determine the consequences of our failures, and we should not let failure discourage us from serving God. Joshua's failure led to significant consequences (a war to defend the Gibeonites in Joshua 10 and the judgment of God in Judges 3), yet Joshua does not give up or waver from the task God has called him to accomplish. His pressing on is quickly rewarded as God assures him of His presence and protection. In reading the Book of Joshua, if you were to jump from chapter 8 to chapter 10 you would not even realize the mistake on Joshua's part. Joshua is leading the people under God's protection in the defeat of Ai in chapter 8. When we read chapter 10, Joshua is leading Israel against the Canaanite coalition under God's protection. His determination to continue to honor God regardless of his past mistakes placed Joshua right back in the center of God's plans for the leader and the children of Israel.

A Challenge for Our Day

- How do you respond in times of personal failure? Do you find yourself looking for others to blame for your faults or sins? Have you had a tendency to excuse your actions based on the conduct of other people, or do you accept responsibility for your own mistakes and quickly seek out repentance and God's forgiveness?
- How much pressure from others are you willing to take in order to maintain your word and personal integrity before God? When you are the target of people complaining, are you more concerned about how they view your actions or how God views your actions?

• In the face of personal mistakes, do you allow the mistakes to paralyze you or sidetrack you from continuing to walk with God? Have you allowed one wrong to compound into multiple mistakes of "not seeking after God" or have you come to the place in your relationship with God where you refuse to let errors stop your forward progress with God and His activity?

Further Study

There are many examples of people God restored during times of failure. While these people may have felt they had ended their usefulness to God or, at the least their role in leadership, their ultimate usefulness was determined by God. However, in these instances we see that in the process of God restoring them, God shaped their character for His purposes.

For further examples to study see:
• Abraham, who, immediately following the promise of God, goes to Egypt and gets in trouble due to his lies (Genesis 12).
• Moses who takes matters in his own hands and ends up having to flee Egypt. Yet, we see God pursue him and begin the process of building his character to lead the children of Israel (Exodus 2–3).
• David, who sinned against God's goodness and is confronted, but is ultimately restored and used by God (2 Samuel 12).

CHAPTER 6

Nicodemus: Character Comes to Light

Because our character is a reflection of our relationship with God, the process of developing character often looks different from one person to another. There are examples in the Scripture of certain people who instantly responded to the call of God and follow after Christ. Some examples of this are the two disciples recorded in John 1:35 and following, or the story of Levi at the tax booth in Mark 2:13 and following. However, I suspect that many of us did not have these kinds of instant responses to Christ. In many cases it may have been a long and drawn-out process before we committed to follow Christ. The process of God developing our character does not simply begin once we have come to know Christ personally, but often begins at a much earlier stage. Many times we may not be aware that God is drawing us toward Himself with the intention to use our life. This was true of a man named Nicodemus recorded in the Gospel of John. While one of the most well-known Scriptures in the Bible (John 3:16) is directly related to his story, he is often overlooked.

Nicodemus is mentioned three times in the Gospel of John. Be careful to notice how he relates to Jesus in each passage as well as the progression as he moves toward taking a stand with Christ. Through the example of Nicodemus, we are challenged not to become disappointed when a person does not follow after Christ or take a stand for Christ immediately. Character does not develop overnight, and there are times we simply need to stand back and watch God and the individual wrestle and process through their personal commitment.

READ JOHN 3:1–21; JOHN 7:45–52; JOHN 19:38–42.

A Closer Look into the Text

When we first meet Nicodemus in John 3, he is described as a Pharisee, a ruler of the Jews. The Pharisees were probably teachers and interpreters of the Torah and were particularly concerned with the laws of purity, Sabbath observations, and tithing. They had constructed a complex set of oral traditions so that they could apply the Law to every situation of life. There are many confrontations between the Pharisees and Jesus because He did not hold to their traditions concerning the observances of the Law, and He also questioned their motivations behind strict adherence to the Law. Nicodemus is called "a ruler of the Jews," which indicates that he was a part of the Sanhedrin which served as the Jewish religious high court, ruling on matters of law for the people. So, as Nicodemus enters the story of the New Testament, he is a prominent figure from a group that is generally unfavorable toward Jesus.

We see something different about Nicodemus. His first words to Jesus were "We know that you are a teacher come from God, for no one can do these signs that you do unless God is with him" (John 3:2 ESV). Notice that he comes to Jesus with an open mind compared to his contemporaries (John 7:45–48), and he did not attribute Jesus' miracles to Satan as others had done (John 8:48; Mark 3:22). It is also important to note that he does not speak alone, but in verse 2 he states, "we know," indicating that there may have been others with him. Most likely, as a teacher of the Law and a member of the Sanhedrin, Nicodemus had students with him as well. It seems that Nicodemus' reference to the miracles is also an implied question of "who are you?" You are a teacher from God, but who are you?

Jesus does not respond to Nicodemus with an answer or explanation of His identity, but rather with a challenge. Nicodemus was a teacher of the Law and had implied an understanding of the ways of God when he said to Jesus: "you must be a teacher from God because of the miracles." However, Jesus' famous words are really a challenge to the man, as the Lord does not reveal His identity, but states that there is only one way to know and see the kingdom of God: "you must be born again." Nicodemus does not understand Jesus' response and, in fact, responds in a rather negative tone that surely a man cannot enter into his mother's womb a second time (3:4). His second reply in verse 9 as to how this could be possible furthers his skepticism about Jesus' comments. Nicodemus was a teacher of the Law and thought that he understood what was required to enter the kingdom of God, but Jesus was presenting a completely different requirement that was unknown to him. If this was the last time to see Nicodemus in John's Gospel, it would be a sad story. The leader, a person of great training and influence, heard the gospel and responded in a skeptical manner. However, this is not the last place we see Nicodemus. While the encounter did not look promising, his story is picked back up in John 7.

The end of John chapter 7 reveals that the leading Pharisees had ordered temple officers to arrest Jesus and bring Him before them. We find the Pharisees upset at the fact that these officers have not brought Jesus before them. Upon questioning them, they discover that the officers had failed in their task due to the manner in which Jesus had spoken. These were not simple guards, but men from the tribe of Levi who served as officers. These men knew the Law and Israel's history and yet had not heard anyone speak as Jesus had. In John 7:45–52 we see a stark contrast between Nicodemus and his fellow members of the Sanhedrin. The Sanhedrin believed the common people listened to Jesus because they were unschooled and did not know the Law. How could anyone who understood the Law be fooled by such an uneducated man? It is at this point that we see that Nicodemus' first encounter with Jesus had not been without effect. For the first encounter, the teacher came to Jesus at night to question Jesus. Surely he must have pondered the encounter because in the face of his colleagues (who are clearly antagonistic toward Jesus) we see Nicodemus launch somewhat of a defense of Jesus. He does not defend Jesus directly; however, he is not willing simply to condemn the Lord without an investigation, as his colleagues had done. In fact, Nicodemus has done much more than his companions; he had met with Jesus to hear Him and find out what He was doing. It appears the leader had not made up his mind at this point. Nicodemus is quickly condemned or mocked by his angered friends (v. 52), but it is important to note that at this second mention, he is at odds with the other Pharisees of his day.

The final mention of Nicodemus in the Gospel of John is significant (19:39). This is only a quick reference, but the note provides an important testimony of a transformation that had taken place in his life. He is mentioned alongside Joseph of Arimathea. Joseph is described as a member of the Sanhedrin (Mark 15:43) who was "a disciple of Jesus, but secretly, for fear of the Jews" (John 19:38 ESV). The reference here of "fear of the Jews" did not refer to all of the Jewish people, but is a reference to the religious leaders. However, he is no longer keeping his faith a secret since he used his influence to meet with Pilate and ask for the body of the Lord. Typically, the body would have been handed over to the deceased's family. However, it would have taken a prominent figure to have the body of Jesus released after such a public and controversial trial and execution. The actions of Joseph would have put him at odds with the ruling Jewish leaders since they were the ones who had instigated the charges and execution.

Both Joseph of Arimathea and Nicodemus would now be the object of much scorn in the social circles in which they traveled. Two Pharisees obtained Jesus' body, provided the large amounts of myrrh and aloes for the preparation of the body, and they placed the body in a new tomb rather than using the traditional burial site for criminals located outside the city. We can see how Joseph who was once a "secret follower" of Christ has now stepped out into the open in his devotion to Christ. However, we see a coming out for Nicodemus as well. Each time he has been mentioned in John's Gospel, it is noted that he came to Jesus at night. Both times he is mentioned—in chapter 7 as well as chapter 19—he is introduced with the reminder, "this is the one who first came to Jesus at night." Do you see the progression of these three accounts? At two levels we can see how he first engaged the Lord at night, then he spoke out in opposition to his colleagues supporting Jesus' opportunity to defend Himself, and (last) we see him taking a stand with a fellow follower of Christ to give the Lord a proper burial in fulfillment of Scripture. However, it is very possible that John was not simply making a reference to the time of day in the first account in chapter 3. John may very well be explaining that the deeds of Nicodemus reveal his moving from darkness to light in line with Jesus' first response to the man in John 3:19–21:

This is the verdict: Light has come into the world, but people loved darkness instead of light because their deeds were evil. . . . But whoever lives by the truth comes into the light, so that it may be seen plainly that what they have done has been done in the sight of God.

The Process of Developing Character

The Gospel of John is the only record we have of Nicodemus in the New Testament. Over time, his story has been overshadowed by the content of Jesus' response in chapter 3 or by the actions of Joseph of Arimathea who is recorded to have spoken to Pilate while Nicodemus provided the materials to prepare Jesus' body. We are sure that most people in the church could give the basic understanding of John 3:16 or remember that a rich person buried Jesus in a tomb, but before you read these passages did you realize that Nicodemus was the one who prompted these important words in John or helped with the burial of Jesus? Yet, John who stated that "there were so many things that Jesus did the world could not contain the books needed to record them" (John 21:25) chose to tell us about Nicodemus—making three mentions of the man.

Nicodemus knew the Law as a Pharisee. He was part of a group that had developed elaborate rules and guidelines on how to interpret and implement the Law into every facet of life. He must have understood the Old Testament teachings concerning God, His ways, and the prophecies concerning the Messiah. In addition, he was a "ruler of the Jews," indicating a part in the Sanhedrin. In this first account, in the face of the skepticism and outright animosity toward Jesus from his fellow Jewish leaders, Nicodemus keeps an open mind toward the ways of God. He does not attribute the miracles of Jesus to Satan as others had done. He does not dismiss the claims of Jesus as just another false Messiah raising support (history records that many others during this time had made this claim). There were actions occurring that he recognized were from God, and yet there were sayings and teachings of Jesus he did not understand. He, however, kept an open mind to the activity of God. The questioning reply to Jesus (3:4, 9) appear to be more out of surprise and confusion at Jesus' response.

The second encounter in chapter 7 provides some understanding on chapter 3. We see a progression in the thinking and actions of Nicodemus related to the Lord. Most certainly the man had not simply dismissed Jesus' words in light of the continued controversy in Jerusalem regarding the Lord. The text does not tells us many details. However, we suggest from chapter 19 that Nicodemus and Joseph of Arimathea would have been in conversation over Jesus, since Joseph is described as a secret follower of Christ. We don't know when they began their conversation concerning Christ, but that they had one is clear from chapter 19. By the second mention of Nicodemus, we see that he has kept an open mind to the ways of God and, while not necessarily committed to Christ, he is beginning to take a stance that conflicts with his fellow Pharisees. What begins in chapter 3 with a question finds completion at the end of John with a full commitment in opposition to his contemporaries and fellow rulers. What is it about this particular Pharisee that stands out from other Pharisees who were clamoring for the death of Christ? We see character that was open to the activity of God even without understanding.

So often we can give up in the face of things unfamiliar or confusing compared to what we know or believe. There are those in the Bible who simply believed and joined right in with Jesus at the beginning of His ministry. However, by chapter 6 of John many have turned away. We have an example of a man who did not hide behind his education, his experience, or what he believed to be true. He could see enough of Jesus' actions to know that God was working; he just didn't understand all that He was doing. However, he does not dismiss or reject Jesus, but continues to keep an open mind and ultimately takes a huge stand for Christ. We don't know, but could it have been Nicodemus who was the encouragement behind Joseph of Arimathea's stand to no longer be a "secret follower" and to take a stand in opposition to the other Pharisees? We see Nicodemus's character as he pursues an understanding regarding Christ. We see one who began in darkness but finds the light by the end of the Book of John. Do we have this same attitude and openness to the activity of God?

The Impact of Character

GOD CAN SHAPE AND TRANSFORM THOSE WHOSE HEARTS ARE OPEN TO HIS ACTIVITIES. Nicodemus clearly did not understand the teachings of Christ in the encounter we read about in chapter 3. These teachings did not match his understanding of the Old Testament that he knew so well. However, Jesus was not teaching a different message divorced from the Hebrew Scriptures; He was correctly living out and fulfilling the Scriptures, which had foretold of Him. The fact that Nicodemus went to Jesus for understanding shows that he did not simply rely on his previous understanding or his colleagues who dismissed the teaching. Rather than arrogance, he showed an openness to listen to Jesus. How often do we encounter God's activity and it does not fit within our own plans or beliefs? Can God provide you with understanding of His activity when you are confused or don't understand? Certainly, but like Nicodemus, you must be open for Him to teach you a new perspective and truth of Himself.

GOD DEVELOPS THE CHARACTER OF THOSE WHO SEEK TO ASK QUESTIONS AND GAIN THEIR OWN UNDERSTANDING OF GOD, RATHER THAN SIMPLY CONFORM TO POPULAR OPINION OR THE PRESSURES OF SOCIETY. Had Nicodemus simply gone with his training and the popular opinion of Jesus he would have found himself in opposition to the activity of God. How ironic this would have been for a man dedicated to living out the law of God in his life, to be in opposition to the very God he was seeking to serve. As we find out through our New Testament, our relationship with God is unique and intensely personal. In the end, was the scorn Nicodemus faced for his openness to hearing Jesus worth the trouble he faced? We think so, as he appears to have met the Light of the world and had the privilege of securing and preparing His body for burial. There is no doubt that the opinion of others as well as the fellowship of others is important. However, we must first seek to understand and know Christ for ourselves, rather than follow the opinions of others about our Lord.

GOD WILL OFTEN JOIN TOGETHER THOSE WHO DESIRE TO FOLLOW AFTER THE KINGDOM. What a fitting way to end the commentary on Nicodemus. He is mocked by his contemporaries for suggesting that the Sanhedrin was unfairly condemning Jesus. The last word concerning Nicodemus is that he and a fellow Pharisee are securing Jesus' body and placing Him in a rich man's tomb (Isaiah 53:9; John 19:41). Often, during the times we are seeking out an understanding of God and His activity, we may feel all alone. There may be times when others mock or quietly question our struggles to understand the activity of God. While the experience may seem to isolate us from others, we can be sure that we are not alone. God knows those around us who love Him and want to serve Him as well. We can be confident that, as God walks with us and develops our character, He will also place others alongside us—for us to encourage as well as to serve as our encouragement.

A Challenge for Our Day

- How open are you to God's activity around your life? If God were to do a "new work" around you or take your life into an unfamiliar setting for ministry would you be open, believe, and follow Him? Because God is always at work around you, be very careful not to simply dismiss situations that may not make sense at first but, through persistent prayer, ask God for His understanding of the situation.

- Are you confident enough in your relationship with God that you are not easily pressured to conform to prevailing opinions around you? Have you made a point of asking God for His perspective and His heart personally rather than simply relying on others' opinions of God and His ways?

- What kind of stand are you willing to make to follow what you know is true concerning God and His ways? Has God invited you to join Him in His work and others are pressuring you not to "get involved"? Have you weighed the cost of bowing to pressures from others as opposed to the joy of serving your Lord?

Further Study

Read Acts 10:1 to 11:18. Look at the way God revealed a "new work" He was going to begin with the Gentiles. Peter understood that God was doing something, but he did not understand what it was and how much out of his comfort zone he would be taken as he met Cornelius. Watch how Peter's response to God put him in conflict with his Jewish colleagues.

CHAPTER 7

Jonah: A Character-Challenged Prophet

Y ou can know the words of God, openly speak about God, and even act like you know God and yet not possess godly character. Words and actions reflect character, but if those outward expressions are empty rituals rather than reflections of the heart of God, then you do not possess godly character. Jonah, the Old Testament prophet, knew the ways and words of God. He was a member of God's covenant people, Israel. He grew up observing the ways of God, and God called him specifically to be His mouthpiece to a people who deserved judgment but to whom God offered mercy. Jonah is an example of someone whose words and actions did not reflect the heart of God but who God used to bring salvation to others.

God's patient guidance of Jonah's life is an example of how God can develop our character to reflect His heart rather than simply religious activity and words.

To Appear Godly Doesn't Mean You Are

Jonah's lack of godly character is not a unique condition among those who claim to know and follow God. Many Americans know of public religious figures who claimed to know God and to live for God, yet, their actions revealed their true character. You may recognize notorious names of religious leaders like David Koresh and Ervil LaBaron who claimed to be God's messengers and who twisted God's words and ways for their personal gain. Other names like Jimmy Swaggart, Jim and Tammy Bakker, and Ted

Haggard cluttered the Internet, tabloids, and evening news to remind us all that we can have large, seemingly successful ministries in the name of God and not possess at that point the character of God. (The good news is that some of these have genuinely repented and begun new lives to serve others in the name of the Lord.) People like these remind us that you can look like you trust and follow the Lord in public, but your character and heart can be far from God.

Jesus confronted this condition of the heart when the religious leaders of His day wanted to know why His disciples did not follow tradition and wash their hands before eating their bread (Matthew 15:2). Jesus turned their question back on them when He asked why they put tradition over the commands of God, citing how the leaders allowed people to choose not to honor their parents in old age by claiming their property was dedicated to God and, therefore, not available to serve their parents' needs (Matthew 15:3–6). Jesus concluded, "It is not what enters into the mouth that defiles the man, but what proceeds out of the mouth, this defiles the man" (Matthew 15:11 NASB). When Peter asked Him to explain, Jesus exposed the core of the issue:

Don't you see that whatever enters the mouth goes into the stomach and then out of the body? But the things that come out of the mouth come from the heart, and these defile you. For out of the heart come evil thoughts, murder, adultery, sexual immorality, theft, false testimony, slander. These are what defile you; but eating with unwashed hands does not defile you.
—MATTHEW 15:17–20 (TNIV)

Jesus taught that the heart is not only the source of our behavior, but that it can drive us to serve ourselves rather than serve God. Our true nature flows from the inside out, beginning with the motives of our heart and becoming outwardly visible in what we do and say. Jesus taught that character begins in the heart, and a heart that has not been transformed by a living, vital relationship with Jesus will only produce self-centered, destructive behaviors—religious behaviors included. You can act religiously and not have the heart of God. Character is a matter of the heart, and we can try to cover our true motives with outward behavior and words that look and sound like godly character, but, in reality, we are only playacting to impress others or to get our way.

What behaviors in your life betray the true motives of your heart?

JONAH WAS A MAN WHO KNEW THE WORDS AND WAYS OF GOD BUT DID NOT HAVE THE CHARACTER OF GOD. The story of Jonah usually gets obscured by the question of whether or not a big fish can really swallow a man, but the message is so much deeper than that. Jonah is a story of a person who knew God, a person God called to share the good news of salvation to a wicked and foreign people. Jonah exposed his true character by refusing to be obedient to God's call. When he eventually did obey God, he mourned the fact that his enemies turned to the Lord! What can we learn from Jonah about how knowing the words and ways of God does not guarantee godly character and about how God can develop our character through His intervention in our lives?

The first indication that Jonah did not share the heart of the One who called him is the fact that he ran from God's command rather than obeying God. When Jonah knew the clear call of God, he literally took a boat in the opposite direction. He did not see the people of Nineveh as God saw them: people who could turn from their wicked ways and trust Him.

Who in your life may God see differently than you do? If God called you to tell them about His love today, how would you respond? We may empathize with Jonah's feelings toward his enemies, but that does not justify his rebellious actions.

Jonah did display some concern for the lives of those who did not share his covenant relationship with God. When a storm almost capsized the boat he hired to take him away from Nineveh, the sailors asked Jonah to call out to his god in order to save the ship and crew. It might be said, "There are no atheists among sailors in a life-threatening storm." Everyone had prayed, and the storm still raged (Jonah 1:5). The AWOL prophet finally admitted—after being chosen by lot, that he was the culprit behind the storm—that his disobedience was the cause of the calamity. He said they should throw him overboard (v. 12). We don't know if this was an altruistic act to save the sailors or a selfish one to end his life. Whatever his motive, the sailors prayed to the God of Jonah and asked forgiveness before they cast the foreigner overboard. The storm stopped when he hit the water. The pagan sailors confessed the power of the God of Israel after they heard Jonah's confession and saw the work of God on the seas. The biblical record says, they "greatly feared the LORD" (v. 16). The sailors trusted Yahweh of Israel to be more powerful and trustworthy than all the gods they had worshipped before.

The irony of this part of the story is that the Lord used Jonah to call pagans to repent and trust the God of Abraham, Isaac, and Jacob. Although he ran from God and God's call on his life, God used Jonah's confession—when forced by the storm and singled out by lot to make that confession—to turn the hearts of the pagan sailors to Him.

GOD DEVELOPS OUR CHARACTER BY RESCUING US, BUT HE MAY ALSO PLACE US IN MORE PAINFUL CIRCUMSTANCES. God sent a "great fish" to rescue Jonah from the sea (1:17). It is hard to decide which situation was worse for Jonah: the storm or the stomach of the fish. The storm was frightening and dangerous enough, but we can only imagine the conditions inside a fish. While in the stomach of the fish, Jonah's heart softened and he rejoiced in the Lord's salvation and restoration of his life. The entire second chapter of his story records his prayer to God. His disobedient heart became one that was submissive to God's leadership and power. He confessed God was his rescuer and that he would faithfully fulfill his vow and worship the Lord (2:9). The combination of events that followed his disobedience led him to return to the One who called him. Like a parent who releases a disobedient child from "time out" after seeing the child's heart has changed, God released Jonah from the fish, which disgorged him onto dry land.

God rescued Jonah from the storm but put him in the belly of a fish. We often pray to God to get us out of a bind (one, like Jonah's, we made for ourselves), and we become upset when things don't turn out the way we think they should. However, simply relieving our pain may not be the way for God to mold our character. Our self-protective and self-centered hearts need guidance beyond our own will to change. We need God to guide and mold us, and that sometimes means remaining in a difficult situation so He can work on our heart. We would rather get out of the heat than be refined by God. Our natural tendencies toward comfort and finding the path of least resistance short-circuit the process for genuine change. We will often say what needs to be said to relieve the pain, but our heart remains in the same sinful mess.

Repentance is not admitting we are wrong in order to avoid the consequences of our sin or God's discipline in our lives. Repentance is a changed heart—and we are not capable of making that change on our own.

GOD CAN USE SUFFERING AND DISCOMFORT TO MOLD OUR CHARACTER AND CALL US BACK TO HIM. Paul, the Apostle, taught that we are to rejoice in our suffering because it "produces endurance, and endurance produces character and character produces hope" (Romans 5:3–4 ESV). Suffering can be God's way of burning away our selfish desires in order to refine us into His likeness. Hope produced by character is God's promise in our suffering. The writer of the Letter to the Hebrews reminds us that "the Lord disciplines those he loves, and he chastens everyone he accepts as his child" (Hebrews 12:6 TNIV). God's intervention in Jonah's life is consistent with what the Bible reveals about His character to discipline those He loves. We agree with the writer, "No discipline seems pleasant at the time, but painful. Later on, however, it produces a harvest of righteousness and peace for those who have been trained by it" (Hebrews 12:11 TNIV). God can use suffering and discomfort as a means to mold our character to that which will ultimately display "righteousness and peace."

SIMPLE OBEDIENCE CAN LEAD OTHERS TO GOD. Jonah preached one of the shortest sermons recorded in the Bible. Its recorded content was that at the end of 40 days, Nineveh will be overthrown (Jonah 3:4). When the reluctant prophet finally obeyed God, he walked through the city proclaiming the message of God. Unexpectedly (to him, but not to God), those who heard the message of God repented and declared their allegiance to the God of Israel. When the king heard the message of possible judgment, he followed his people's example and put on sackcloth and ashes and declared that the city must repent. The people trusted the message of God and reasoned that if they changed how they lived, God would change His mind and "relent and with compassion turn from his fierce anger so that we will not perish" (v. 9). This is the second time in the story where pagans cried out to the God of Israel after Jonah finally obeyed the Lord.

Simple obedience is God's portal to changing the hearts of others. We think we know what it takes for another person to turn to the Lord, but this is foolish pride. God is at work in every life through relationships and experiences. Given that reality and our inability to know the hearts of others, God calls us to be witnesses to Him in word and deed. The Holy Spirit will convict and change hearts. So, as in Jonah's case, our faithful witness—one sentence, well-timed—to a person or group of people may be all it takes for God to produce heart change in the life of another.

When has God used your simple obedience to be His life-changing bridge in the life of another? How have you been obedient to God's call on your life to be His witness to others?

OUR RESPONSE TO GOD'S FORGIVENESS OF OTHERS REVEALS OUR TRUE CHARACTER. Jonah's attitude toward the people of Nineveh never matched God's love toward them. When the people responded in repentance to the message of God, Jonah became angry (Jonah 4:1). He knew the character of God, and he knew that God would respond compassionately toward the people if they repented. His confession carries the revealed character of God in the Bible: "I knew that you are a gracious and compassionate God, slow to anger and abounding in love, a God who relents from sending calamity" (v. 2; Psalm 103:8). God acted according to His character. Jonah did too. Jonah admitted that the reason he headed in the opposite direction of his call was because he knew God would act according to His character toward the people. The prophet childishly asked God to kill him rather than allow him to see his enemies live (4:3). To which God answered in today's jargon, "Really?"

Jonah continued his childish behavior by climbing a hill east of the city to see if God would change His mind. When God sent a plant to cover where Jonah sat and provide shade from the hot sun, the prophet became happy. God then sent a worm to kill the plant, and Jonah sat again in the heat. When the prophet complained, God asked him how he could be so upset about a little plant when he had nothing to do with its growth or destruction and not be even more concerned about Nineveh, which was an enormous city (4:10–11). Jonah cared more about his comfort and the destruction of his enemies than the Lord's display of compassion for so many people. God cared about the people. God also cared about Jonah or He would have not taken the time to be compassionate toward the infantile attitudes and actions of his prophet. God responded to both the enemies of Israel and a disobedient prophet in line with His true character.

Authentic biblical character reflects the heart of God. When God forgives or shows compassion to those we are convinced do not deserve it, our response to His forgiveness reveals whether or not our character matches that of the God we say we love. Jonah did not reflect the character of God at any time in this story. He consistently showed his true character as he disobeyed God and wished for his own death over Nineveh's salvation. Yet, God consistently developed the character of Jonah by taking him off the boat, putting him in a fish, and displaying an object lesson with a plant and a worm in the heat of the day. Although the prophet was obedient only when forced to do so, God patiently gave him opportunities to repent.

God calls us to love others and extend His forgiveness to all people. Our sinfulness and self-centeredness keep us from demonstrating God's character. We are more like Jonah than God when it comes to being obedient and reflecting God's character, and that may be the point of Jonah's story. God has called us to be a "blessing to the nations" and to demonstrate the character of God to all people. We, however, live out of our sin-jaded character. God, on the other hand, chooses to develop our character while revealing His. God truly is "slow to anger" (4:2). Praise Him!

A Challenge for Our Day

- Nineveh represented a people group who did not respect the Lord. Who do you know in your community who does not respect the Lord? Write some of their names here.
- Jesus reflected the heart of the Father when He called His disciples to be "witnesses" in their world. That call is valid for your life as a follower of Jesus. How have you been a witness to God's love and forgiveness to others?
- How have you been like Jonah? Write out a confession on a piece of paper or journal.
- In what ways has God patiently disciplined you in order to guide you to obedience?

Further Study

Take time to dig a little deeper into the life of Jonah to learn more about how God molded his character and used his life to help others trust Him.

- In Acts 10:1 to 11:18, God asked Peter to take the good news to the Gentiles through very unique visions and circumstances. Take time to read this passage. Compare Peter's response to God with Jonah's response to God.
- Find the Book of Jonah in your Bible. What other books surround it? What was going on in the life of Israel during the days of Jonah?
- Reread the story and make a list of those actions by God that reflect His character. Review the story for those things that demonstrate Jonah's true character.

CHAPTER 8

Mary, Mother of Jesus: Confident Assurance

A friend called me (Gene) one day and said he needed to talk. When we met at a local coffee shop, he told me his 15-year-old daughter was pregnant. He shared the circumstances surrounding the relationship and that the family had decided to keep the baby, no matter what the cost. I asked him to let the church help and to let us walk alongside them through this challenge. The teenage mother remained in school and involved in our church. She graduated from high school and attended the local junior college, confidently assured this was the path God wanted her to follow. Her daughter is as much a part of our fellowship as any other growing newborn. The family members remain active in our church, and we now partner with the program in our local school district that helps teenage parents get their high school diplomas and find jobs. Some of our members are mentors to the young mothers and fathers, and we host monthly meetings to give the students the skills and items they need to raise a healthy child. An unwanted pregnancy and the faith of a young mother led to the birth of a wonderful child and a ministry to serve others in similar situations.

God developed the character of that family and our church with that unexpected pregnancy. Because of that experience, we are on the frontlines of caring for the unborn and serving their parents in the name of Jesus.

Centuries ago a teenager, engaged to be married, came to her parents and announced she was pregnant. That teenage girl was Mary, the mother of Jesus. Have you ever wondered how Mary's parents responded to her announcement? How did her neighbors and friends react to the news? Did the story of the angel Gabriel's intervention help ease the tension?

What thoughts raced through the teenager as she faced her family and friends? We do not know the answers to those questions, but we do have preserved in Scripture how Mary responded to the announcement and how God used her to bring about the birth of God's only begotten Son, Jesus.

God Invites Us to Join Him

In the biblical story of Mary we can see that *God develops character by inviting us to join Him in His plan to redeem the world through Christ Jesus.* Mary did not choose to be part of what God was doing in history to bring about the birth of the Messiah. God, in His providential love, chose her according to His purposes to join Him in His redemptive plans. As we observe Mary's responses to God's call on her life, we learn of her character and the character of God who called her to this wonderful journey of faith.

Take a moment to read the biblical account of the birth announcement in Luke 1:26–38. Interact with the passage by writing questions that may come to your mind or facts you may want to study later.

God sent Gabriel to reveal His intentions to Mary. The angel of the Lord began his message by stating that she had found "favor" with God (Luke 1:28). This word signaled God's pleasure or blessing upon a person or a people. What was it about Mary that that caused God to choose her above all others to bear His only begotten Son? We can't know the heart of God fully for He is God, but we know her promised marriage to Joseph who was in the lineage of King David played a part. We also know she was a faithful member of Israel because she had followed the accepted traditions of marriage and purity.

Beyond the clear connections to God's stated plans, we can wonder if

God saw in her character a faithful assurance that she would trust God no matter the extreme nature of His announcement. Mary's unwavering trust in God was the basis of her character which she displayed as she became a central part of God's plan for His people. Her faithful assurance allowed her to humble herself to do whatever God asked her to do.

Being the mother of the promised Son of God was a huge honor. Who would not want to accept that place in God's history? But Mary was a common girl from a common family with no ties to visible power and prestige, and she was not married! What human reasons would lead anyone to choose her as the earthly mother of God's only Son? God does not always choose who we would pick to bring His purposes to reality.

God clearly saw Mary's character would not fail to trust Him no matter the request He made of her, and this task was beyond her comprehension. Read what Gabriel told her:

You will conceive and give birth to a son, and you are to call him Jesus. He will be great and will be called the Son of the Most High. The Lord God will give him the throne of his father David, and he will reign over the house of Jacob forever; his kingdom will never end.
—Luke 1:31–33 (TNIV)

What a God-sized task! God surely saw in this young girl a faithful and trusting heart or He would not have asked her to perform this act of faith. God tested Mary's character by inviting her to participate in His redemptive work through Jesus, God's Son.

God develops our character in much the same way. None of us will bear Jesus. That was Mary's unique role in God's plans, but God does ask us to participate in His redemptive story. Scripture makes it clear that God has given those of us who trust Jesus "the ministry of reconciliation," and we are "ambassadors for Christ" (2 Corinthians 5:18–20). We also are witnesses of Jesus' resurrection who are sent to our neighbors and to "the ends of the earth" to tell the Good News of Jesus (Acts 1:8). God has come to each of us who trust Jesus and has asked us to invest our time, talents, and treasures in people and projects that yield eternal value. As Paul reminds us, our lives are not our own, for we have been bought with a price (1 Corinthians 6:19–20). Christian character is built upon our faithful assurance of who we are as a result of our relationship with Jesus.

God calls us to join Him in His redemptive plans, and our response to that call is a point where He can develop our character. If we could see our lives as God sees them—as salt-and-light servants whom God uses to change the hearts of others—we would realize the kind of character required to live such a life. We would not take lightly the places God has invited us to join Him in His redemptive purposes. We would focus more on the relationships of family and friends God has given us to influence for eternity than on our nine to five jobs. We would see where we live, work, and play as our missions fields to share the good news of Jesus.

Have you considered God's invitation to join Him in the eternal, global "ministry of reconciliation?" Do you trust God enough to humble yourself and your resources to His purposes so He can develop your character and use your life to help others trust Jesus as their Rescuer and Leader?

That's Impossible!

Mary's story also teaches us that *God develops character by challenging us with the impossible.* God told Mary through Gabriel that she would conceive a child without the aid of a man and that she would give birth to a son who was the long-awaited Messiah. Mary trusted the angel's message, but she also displayed authentic character by asking an obvious question, "How will this be . . . since I am a virgin?" (Luke 1:34). She had the integrity to ask what was on her mind in order to understand more fully God's seemingly impossible request of her. *Faithful assurance is not blind acceptance.* Mary did not question why God asked her to do this, nor did she argue the implications of God's call on her marriage and family. She knew the ancient stories of how faithful, barren women like Sarah and Hannah had become pregnant, but she could have never imagined what the angel told her.

Questions are part of authentic faith. Take Moses, for example. He trusted God, but he had questions about how God would use him to lead Israel's tribes out of Egypt. (Read Exodus, chapters 3 and 4, for his dialogue with God.) Moses asked many more recorded questions than Mary, and God enlisted him to deliver Israel from bondage. Moses was not alone in his questions when confronted with God's plan for his life. Gideon wondered how he could be God's choice to rescue Israel from its enemies (Judges 6:12–17). He was the youngest in his tribe, and it was the "weakest" of all of the others. And he reminded the messenger of God that God's enemies constantly overran his farmland. How could he be God's "mighty warrior?" When God asks us to do what seems impossible from our human perspective, God allows time for us to ask questions.

God develops our character through such a *dialogue of faith.* Mary could not fathom being pregnant without being with a man. Moses and Gideon could not see good reasons why they would be worthy of the task God asked them to complete. God's servants are not afraid to humbly ask questions from their limited, human perspective, and God is able to answer them.

You may not think such faith is required of you since God has not asked you to be the mother of His only Son, the deliverer of His people, or a mighty warrior to defeat His enemies. But maybe God has called you to forgive a brother from whom you have been estranged for years. What about the impossible task of standing before the city council to advocate for the poor in your city? That may feel like Moses standing before the Pharaoh of Egypt. Caring for the needs of special needs children and their families in your school district with dwindling funds may also seem impossible. And, what can you do when God calls you to go to the area of a natural disaster to help rebuild homes for families there? God is always calling His people to engage a fallen world to share the Good News of Jesus Christ. Honest questions and faithful assurance are the keys to doing what God has called us to do.

Let It Happen as You Say

When Gabriel explained how Mary's pregnancy would happen, she displayed the depth of her character by being obedient with no further questions. Although we are sure she did not understand fully how the conception would happen—a mystery we accept by faith to this day—she trusted the angel's words and humbled herself to God's plan. Gabriel reminded her (and us) that "nothing is impossible with God" (Luke 1:37). And, as evidence for His claim, He told her that Elizabeth, her older relative, was pregnant after being barren her entire life. When Mary heard the angel's words, the young girl humbly replied, "I am the Lord's slave. . . . May it be done to me according to your word" (Luke 1:38 HCSB). Mary confessed her humble status before the Lord and her willingness to trust God's message, no matter the consequences. Later, when she sang her song to magnify the

Lord for His gracious acts, she confessed aloud that the Lord had "looked with favor on the humble condition of His slave" (v. 48).

Mary displayed character built upon the faithful assurance that God's Word was true and upon a humble perspective about who she was before the Lord. God developed those attributes of her character by asking her to join in His redemptive plans and to trust Him with the apparent impossibility of the virgin birth. Mary is an example of how God develops the character of those He calls.

We learn from Mary that obedience is trust in action. Mary acted on her faith. She immediately went to her relative Elizabeth and shared her story of the angel visit. What a scene it must have been after they greeted one another and began to tell the stories of how God had come to them and revealed His plan to them. No wonder Mary was filled with song! God's words were true in Elizabeth's life, and she knew they would soon be fully realized. *Faithful assurance in God's Word leads to faithful obedience to God's Word.* A hallmark of biblical character is humble obedience to the Word of God. Through such obedience God accomplishes His purposes to provide redemption for the world to Himself in Christ Jesus.

The unexpected pregnancy of the teenage girl in our church tested the character of God's people. Yet, through their faithful assurance of God's Word to serve those in need and to protect and nurture life, they were obedient to God's Word. They cared for and accepted the family, mother, and child in the name of Jesus. It was not easy for anyone involved, but they honored God through their caring obedience and humble hearts. The birth of the child in our church was nothing like that of Mary's, but it caused the same responses from God's people to what He had called them to do.

A Challenge for Our Day

• Who have you known who has faced an unexpected situation in life? How did you and your family respond?

• What is God clearly calling you to do, but you consider it impossible from your perspective? What questions have you asked God about His call?

• How have you demonstrated a humble trust in God's Word although it may seem impossible or too painful?

• When have you been obedient to God's leadership in your life? Write out some examples in your journal to build your assurance that God is true to His Word.

Further Study

Read the story of God's call on Mary's life from the perspective of a parent. Now, reread it from the perspective of the teenager, Mary, then from Elizabeth's perspective. Ask God to reveal other characteristics of her character we have not discussed.

• Read an article from a Bible dictionary, encyclopedia, or study Bible on the life of Mary. Look up "virgin birth" to learn of the importance of this doctrine to every Christian's faith.

• Read other biblical accounts (such as Luke 2:41–50; John 2:1–11; Acts 1:14) to learn more about Mary, the mother of Jesus, God's only Son.

CHAPTER 9

John Mark: Character Makes a Comeback

Often when we hear of people quitting something they started, we tend to write them off as losers not capable of finishing the job. Our culture places high value on completing an assigned task, and those who can't follow through are often asked to go somewhere else. God frequently chooses moments of perceived failure and what follows as the path to mold us more into the image of His Son and for us to experience a deepened relationship with Him. John Mark—we know him as Mark—is a person God molded into a faithful servant leader, although he failed one of the best known characters of the New Testament, the Apostle Paul.

Depending on where we read about John Mark in the New Testament, we may regard him as a hero of the faith or as one who sheepishly quit because things got too hard. By the end of the story, however, we discover that while he did not get it right the first time, in the end he made a huge and lasting contribution to the expanding movement of Jesus. John Mark is an example of how God develops character in those who allow Him to work through what may be painful and embarrassing choices.

Meet John Mark

We meet John Mark in his home at a prayer meeting for the imprisoned Peter, the leader of the early church (Acts 12:12). John Mark's mother, Mary, was a member of the Jerusalem church. They had gathered to pray for Peter's release. Herod, the puppet governor, had put Peter in jail because of his bold witness for Jesus. John Mark was part of that anxious group of Christ followers who prayed for the release of Peter and soon experienced his miraculous appearance at the front door. John Mark's home was where he gained firsthand experience of the power of God through prayer.

John Mark grew up in a home built upon the teachings of God. He grew up learning Scripture and practicing the ways of God. He came to trust Jesus as the fulfillment of God's promises and the Savior of Israel. Young John Mark presumably knew firsthand the story of Jesus (and may have known Jesus Himself). He witnessed the presence of the Holy Spirit in the lives of those who trusted Jesus and experienced the miracle of God sending the Holy Spirit to form the church at Pentecost. He knew many who were baptized and who followed Jesus as the Messiah, and he saw their numbers grow every day. When he saw Peter standing at his door, he realized the power of prayer among God's people. God used a godly mother, a nurturing home, the community of faith, and the Holy Spirit to mold the character of this young follower of Jesus. We have no indication early in the story that he would not be faithful to God's leadership in his life.

Read Acts 11:27 through Acts 12:25 to get the full story of John Mark's early life.

After the death of Herod, Barnabas and Saul, who had been previously sent by the church in Antioch with a gift to help the poor in Jerusalem (Acts 11:30), returned to Antioch, taking John Mark with them (Acts 12:25). During his trip to Antioch, he came under the tutelage of the two prominent leaders of the early church, Paul and Barnabas. John Mark had heard of the explosive growth of the new church in Antioch, and he was about to experience it for himself. Barnabas and Paul, who had taught the new Christians for over a year in Antioch, saw something in John Mark that caused them to invite him to join in their ministry to build the church across ethnic, religious, and social barriers in the Syrian town. The two mentors taught him the things of God and how God's New Covenant people could expand to other communities and across all barriers. When the Holy Spirit prompted the church to set apart Barnabas and Saul for the "work to which [He had] called them," they took John Mark with them (Acts 13:1–3).

There can be little doubt that John Mark's time spent with Paul and Barnabas made a huge impact on his character development. Their teaching, example, and passion for Christ allowed him to grow in his trust and understanding of Jesus and His call on his life. Paul, who had been a Pharisee and had a personal encounter with the risen Lord, taught Mark the full story of God's work in the world to bring salvation to all through Jesus. Simply sitting under the Apostle Paul's teaching for over a year gave him insights into Scripture and the ways of God few others had experienced. Barnabas, with his encouraging spirit and open heart to the things of God, showed Mark the ways of God among the unique gathering of the church in Antioch. The young missionary was equipped and called to join God on mission in places and among people he had never known before.

Deserter!

As we live life, we make choices—choices that impact us in the present and future as well as choices that change how others relate to us. Character is both exposed and built when we make these life-changing choices. This was true during John Mark's trip with Barnabas and Paul on the first journey to spread the message of Jesus beyond the Jewish population of Israel, taking the gospel message "to the ends of the earth" (Acts 1:8). He experienced the power of the Holy Spirit, saw people trust Jesus as the Messiah, and continually sat under the leadership and teaching of Paul and Barnabas, the leaders of this world-wide mission. He also experienced the resistance some religious leaders had to this new belief about Jesus as the Messiah.

Something, however, happened on the Island of Cyprus that caused John Mark to leave the missionary team and return to his home in Jerusalem (Acts 13:13). Luke, the writer of Acts, is brief in his description of Mark's departure and gives no details as to why he left. We don't know if he went home to care for his mother who may have become ill, or if the experiences with the proconsul Serigus Paulus and sorcerer Elymas overwhelmed him and he returned to the safety of the life of faith he knew in Jerusalem.

Read Acts 13:4–13 to know the full account of events that led to John Mark's leaving. Would you have left?

We can only speculate what made Mark leave, but his decision would become cause for Paul not to invite him on another trip with him, and it would cause a rift in Paul and Barnabas's relationship. Leaving when he did does not mark a flaw in the young missionary's character. It does not say that he could not finish what he started. Only when we know the full story of the circumstances that led to his departure can we make a fair judgment about his character. We can, however, evaluate how others responded to his choice to return home.

John Mark's choice had lasting implications in his relationships with his mentors. We don't know what was said at his leaving. Hurtful things may have been said or not. Either way, this experience could have ended his involvement in the global work of the church. We will learn later that Paul considered Mark a deserter for leaving to go home when he did. This negative assessment of his actions could have had a devastating effect on Mark's character. While he was away from the front lines of engagement in ministry, he had time to reflect, and it gave God an opportunity to further mold his character.

We all know what it feels like to be rejected by someone or turned down for a position we saw ourselves as worthy to hold. The time after such a rejection can be used to mold our character positively or negatively. Disappointment can lead to bitterness and regret, and we can find ourselves despondent toward any future opportunities. On the other hand, a choice to make a change, although negatively evaluated by others, can become a season of reflection and a deepened relationship with God. The text is silent on how John Mark spent his time while he was away from the frontlines of the mission to the Gentiles. We can assume John Mark used this time wisely based on the final outcome of his life.

A Rift of Biblical Proportions

We never know how our decisions will affect others in the future. John Mark's choice to leave the two missionaries became a catalyst for the duo's separation. Such a divorce between ministry partners had not been seen in the church up until this time. Shock waves of the news had an impact on the perception of how biblical relationships are to work—even until today. How could such a thing happen between men whose character clearly reflected the person of Christ?

Barnabas and Saul, who went by the name Paul after meeting the proconsul on Cyprus (Acts 13:9), completed their first journey to carry the story of Jesus to ethnic groups beyond Judaism. After a conference to hammer out the details of how non-Jewish people would become followers of Jesus, Paul and Barnabas were ready to make a second journey. Barnabas wanted to take John Mark along with them again (Acts 15:37). Paul, now the fiery leader, refused to take John Mark with them "because he had deserted them in Pamphylia and had not continued with them in the work" (Acts 15:38). From Paul's perspective, John Mark had failed and did not deserve to make a second trip with them. The embattled leader needed men and women he could depend upon no matter how difficult things became. Paul did not see what Barnabas saw in Mark. Surely the sting of this leader's assessment of John Mark burned deeply in his heart. We have no record of the rejected missionary's response to Paul, but we know that Barnabas believed in him to the point that he separated from his long-time partner in ministry and took John Mark with him to his homeland of Cyprus (Acts 15:39).

Have you ever had a leader you respected no longer want to work with you? Or, have you had a leader who has stood up for you when others labeled you a failure? God uses times like these to mold your character. If you allow the assessment of others to determine your identity, you will never become the person of character God has created you in Christ Jesus to be. Whether the CEO or janitor, your identity is in Christ and *that* identity is the foundation upon which your character is built. The Bible reminds us we are God's adopted children in Christ Jesus and, if we are his children, we are heirs and, therefore, co-heirs with Christ (Romans 8:16–17). John Mark trusted Jesus to be his leader and rescuer, and no matter what a respected leader labeled him, we will see that he continued to serve when given the chance. Christlike character withstands the labels placed on our lives by others.

We don't know the backstory of John Mark's life after Paul declared him unfit for ministry with him. But, we do know he did not quit serving and that he eventually reengaged with his mentor, and they were reconciled.

The character of Christ grew in his heart even after he was rejected. Rather than holding a grudge against his senior leader, we will see that he submitted to the leadership of Barnabas and continued his ministry. What Paul labeled a failure, God used to mold Mark's character into what was needed to make a lasting contribution to the work of Christ around the world and for generations to come.

Reconciliation Restores the Wounded Heart

We do not hear of John Mark again in the Book of Acts. Luke leaves him on the Island of Cyprus with his mentor and cousin, Barnabas, doing the work of the Lord in that place. We do hear of him in the unlikely places in letters to churches written by Paul himself. Paul, who had labeled John Mark a deserter, came back in contact with the young Christian sometime after their separation, and the senior missionary began to partner with Mark in ministry again. We know this from how Paul addressed Mark in his letters to others. For example, from prison, Paul wrote the church in Colosse, and he sent them greetings from "Mark, the cousin of Barnabas" (Colossians 4:10). Mark, the deserter, was now with the aging missionary who believed a greeting from him would encourage the church. Paul also mentioned Mark's presence with him in his short letter to Philemon (v. 24). After a few years of separation from the one who had declared him unfit for service, Mark once again served with his mentor. Maybe during a visit to Paul in prison his former mentor forgave Mark and they were reunited in ministry. We do not know how the reconciliation took place, but Mark demonstrated God-like character if he made the initial move to go to the one who had rejected and labeled him. This act alone made it possible for the elder statesmen to demonstrate God's life-changing grace in his own life.

Paul wrote in his correspondence to Corinth that all who followed Jesus had been given the "ministry of reconciliation" (2 Corinthians 5:16–19). We are no longer to view people "from a worldly point of view," he wrote, but as the "new creation" we are in Christ. Paul and John Mark exhibited how reconciliation works in real life. Both were able to forgive one another and be reconciled to one another so God could work in their lives as a team again. If either had kept a grudge against the other or had not demonstrated Christlike character, these two leaders may not have ever worked together again. What a loss to God's work that would have been!

Have you ever experienced biblical reconciliation? Have you made the first step toward forgiving someone who has maligned you? Such gracious forgiveness and reconciliation is impossible without character like Christ. Scripture teaches us that God was pleased "through him [Christ] to reconcile to himself all things, whether things on earth or things in heaven, by making peace through his blood, shed on the cross" (Colossians 1:20). Paul later wrote "that God was reconciling the world to himself in Christ, not counting people's sins against them" (2 Corinthians 5:19). Those who have the character of God take the first step toward reconciliation and restoration. Whether Paul or John Mark made the first move is not really the point. The fact is two men who were estranged in relationship forgave one another and reconciled their differences in order to be useful to God once more.

By the time Paul was imprisoned in Rome and near the end of his ministry, we read in Paul's second letter to his protégé, Timothy, "get Mark and bring him with you, because he is helpful to me in my ministry" (2 Timothy 4:11). Mark was no longer simply *with* Paul. The aged missionary now labeled John Mark "helpful." From "deserter" to "helpful" marked the character development of this young follower of Jesus—and Paul was sending for him! John Mark may not have gotten things right the first time, but in the end he became the man God created him to be in Christ Jesus.

Both Paul and John Mark exhibited the character of Christ in their hearts when they were reconciled after their separation. We don't have a record of when or how this happened, but we can read how Paul welcomed the young man back into the mission to the Gentiles from his letters to others. Forgiveness and reconciliation are hallmarks of Christlike character.

Even "Failures" Can Make a Difference

The Scriptures go silent regarding John Mark after Paul's letters. But that is not the end of his story. We know from the early church tradition that Mark was the writer of the New Testament book that bears his name, The Gospel According to Mark. Church history tells us that while in Rome he wrote down the preaching of Peter and spent time with Paul. Most scholars believe his short book is the earliest, complete written account of the life of Jesus, which we call a Gospel. If this is so, it means God used someone whom a prominent leader in the church called a "deserter" (and who also refused to work with him for a time) to preserve the life-changing story of Jesus. Continuing with this idea of how we obtained the Gospels, Mark's story of Jesus is the bedrock upon which the other two Gospels by Matthew and Luke were written and which formed the foundation of faith of all who follow Jesus today. John Mark's record of Jesus' ministry is foundational for our knowledge of Jesus today.

Neal Cole in his book, *Organic Leadership*, writes that he found "the three things that Jesus views as crucial to the success of his followers" are "faithfulness, fruitfulness, and finishing well". We agree that Cole has assessed the biblical record well and when applied to John Mark, the youthful missionary stumbled at faithfulness to God's call on his life early in his ministry, but he lived a life of fruitfulness, and he finished well. Cole concludes, "How you live your life is important. How you finish your life is most important." John Mark is an example of finishing well after he did not get it right the first time.

Even if we do not get things right the first time we try, God patiently uses all of our experiences and the people He places in our lives to mold us into the likeness of His Son, Jesus. John Mark is a reminder that Christlike character does not always register as earthly or even kingdom success, but it will be the foundation for a life that finishes well according to God's standards.

A Challenge for Our Day

- When have you experienced a season of life that someone else labeled as failure but God used to mold your character into His likeness? What were your initial reactions to the experience? If there has been time to reflect upon it, in what ways have you seen God use that time to change your heart toward Him and others?

- Who are the leaders in your life from whom you have received training and guidance? How have they prepared you for the service God has called you to complete?

- Have you experienced a broken relationship and restored it through Christlike reconciliation? If so, recount the story prayerfully and thank God for leading you to heal that relationship. If not, are there any relationships in which you need to reconcile with the person who hurt you? Ask God for the strength to live out "the ministry of reconciliation" he has given you in Christ.

Further Study

Take time to dig a little deeper into the life of John Mark to learn more about how God molded his character and used his life to help others trust Jesus.

- Review John Mark's early life and how God used his mother, home, and community of faith to mold his character.
- Read all of Acts 13 to see the circumstances surrounding John Mark's experiences with Barnabas and Saul.
- Reflect on the separation of Barnabas and Paul, and write a list of benefits that resulted from the team's division (Acts 15:36–41).

CHAPTER 10

Jesus and the Disciples: Growing Pains

T

he hardest job either of us has been given was to mold the character of our children. This is not because our children were difficult but because molding a life takes so much time, energy, emotional investment, and effort. Developing character is not done in days but in years and, as long as we are in relationship with our children, we will have influence upon their character.

Developing character is more like nurturing a child into adulthood than completing an online course on "How to Develop Character" in a college-level psychology class. The primary differences are the relationship between the parent and child versus the teacher and student and the years spent training the child, rather than the weeks it takes to finish a course. We can accumulate knowledge about character through reading and study, but until we are in relationship with God and fellow disciples of Jesus, we will never display godly character.

Jesus is our primary example of how to develop godly character in the lives of others. His three-year ministry on earth with His disciples is a laboratory for character development that we can observe and which we can apply to today's followers of Jesus. Let's take a look at how Jesus called His first followers and how He molded their character.

Take a moment to read Mark 1:14–20 to see the biblical account of Jesus' call to some of His disciples.

Change How You Live! The Kingdom Is Near.

Before Jesus called his first disciples to join Him on mission, He let people know He had come to announce the "gospel of God" and establish the kingdom of God. How was this so? He told them time was filled up, or fulfilled, for such things and that "the kingdom of God is near" (Mark 1:15). What did this mean? People were to "repent" and "believe the good news" He brought to them. The word "repent" literally means to "change one's mind," but there is more to it than simply changing your mind. *Repentance means a change of heart that ultimately leads to a new way of life.* In essence, Jesus said, "Because the time is ripe and the kingdom of God is near, you need to change how you see things and how you live." Repentance that prepares the heart for tangible, authentic change is the first step to allowing Jesus to develop our character.

Jesus then called people to believe this "good news" or "gospel" (v. 15). The good news was His message about the kingdom of God, which referred to the reign of God in people's hearts; and His demonstration of God's reign through His life. The word for "believe" is more about trust in a person than merely to believe an idea. For example, almost all of us believe there is a God, but a smaller number trust God enough to live as He commands for us to live. Jesus requires we trust Him, not just believe facts about Him, in order to become a follower. These are the initial conditions of discipleship: a changed heart and trust in Jesus to be our Rescuer and Leader.

Called to Follow

Jesus walked by the Sea of Galilee one day and saw Simon and his brother Peter casting their nets. They were fisherman whom Jesus called to follow and to learn about the kingdom of God from Him. Mark tells us Jesus said for them to come and follow Him, and He would show them how to "fish for people" (Mark 1:17 TNIV). He used something the two brothers did day in and day out to describe what He would show them how to do if they would follow Him. He went farther down the shore and called two other brothers, James and John (vv. 18–20). They left their nets with the hired hands and followed Jesus.

Jesus' analogy of fishing for people has several implications for us when applied to character development. Fishing implies learned skills, experience, as well as knowledge. While being a disciple at its core means being a learner, Jesus was more interested in training His followers in a way of life rather than simply giving them more information about the rules and laws of God. These men knew the facts of their religion. Since they were boys, they had undoubtedly memorized the Torah and Psalms, and they had observed the festivals and traditions with their parents. As grown men, they practiced these things with their families. Jesus called them to learn the skills of how to live under God's rule, not to become students of God. Dallas Willard wrote that the better image for disciple is "apprentice" rather than learner. An apprentice is with someone in order to be like him or her or to learn a skill from that person. Willard wrote, "If I am Jesus' disciple that means I am with Him to learn from Him how to be like Him." An intentional relationship with the purpose of becoming like Jesus is the foundation of being a disciple of Jesus. *We in the West have turned Jesus' trade school of discipleship into a university of ideas about God.* Jesus wanted to develop their character; not give them a degree in religion.

Jesus' method of training was what we call the "follow me" method. Jesus told the fishing brothers to drop their current way of life, come and follow Him, and He would "make" them "fishers of men." Remember the call to repent and how it meant to change one's heart and mind so he or she could live differently as God's people? This meaning is wrapped up in Jesus' call to Simon and Andrew. He called them to repent from—change their hearts about—their current way of life and trust Him enough to drop the life they had formed and follow Him into a new way of living. They would then learn the skills of "fishing for people" as Jesus demonstrated the "at-hand" kingdom of God.

What are some skills you have learned by following Jesus through the pages of Scripture, in community with others, and with the guidance of the Holy Spirit? Are you more like Jesus in what you say and do now than when you first met Him?

Jesus' School of Character Development

What did Jesus' "follow Me" method of training look like? When we observe His life, we see that Jesus called His disciples, *taught* them, *modeled* for them, and *empowered* them to live as kingdom-of-God people. When the two sets of fishing brothers dropped their nets and followed Jesus, they entered *Jesus' school of character development*. He changed their hearts, and those changed hearts resulted in a new way of life. Let's examine how He did this.

JESUS CALLED THEM. We observed above how Jesus called His first disciples to join Him in telling and showing others the "near kingdom of God" He embodied. Jesus met the men where they lived and used images with which they were familiar to challenge them to change how they thought and lived in order to follow Him. Jesus called them to change their lives, follow Him, and learn from Him this new way of life.

A life on mission with God begins with a call to follow Him. That call can come in various forms. When we observe the biblical record, we see the many ways God called people out of their normal lives to join Him on mission. God called out to Moses from a burning bush. God sent an angel to call Gideon who led the tribes of Israel in defeat of their enemies. God sent Gabriel to announce to Mary she would bear the Son of God. The risen Christ met Saul of Tarsus on the road to Damascus in a shining light, and God called Peter to cross the threshold of social and religious barriers by entering Cornelius's house and seeing a vision of animals in a sheet. While these are memorable and somewhat spectacular ways of calling, God has revealed His purposes in Scripture. No one who reads the teachings of Jesus can say, "I don't know what God is calling me to do with my life." Passages like the Great Commandment (Mark 12:28–34) and Great Commission (Matthew 28:18–20) reveal God's desire for those who trust Jesus. Start with these clear commands, and you will soon answer the question, "What is God's will for my life?"

Why is the calling so important to godly character development? Both of us have stressed the importance of call in our walk with the Lord and in our lives. We wrote, "Your response to God's call is the most transforming event in your life—all else flows from it." When you encounter God's call on your life, and decide to say yes to Him, like the fishing brothers, your life will change forever. When Jesus calls you to join Him on mission as His disciple, how you respond reveals the heart of your character.

In what ways have you sensed God's clear call on your life? How have you responded to that call? What is different in your life because of His call?

JESUS TAUGHT THEM. Training includes knowledge. That's why plumbers study manuals and take qualifying exams along with learning how to solder pipes together. Jesus taught His disciples about what the kingdom of God looked like and how they were to behave under the reign of God. Matthew 10, for example, is an extended teaching of Jesus to His disciples. Before He sent them out to tell and demonstrate the power of God, He gave them specific instructions on how to live as His sent ones (Matthew 10:5–42). For example, He taught them what to say: "As you go, proclaim this message: 'The kingdom of heaven has come near'" (v. 7). He taught them what to take and not take with them, and He warned them of the dangers they would face as His apostles (vv. 9, 10, 16, 17).

Teaching is essential to developing character. This is why regular times of reading, listening to and dialogue with a teacher who follows the Lord are so important in our character development. This does not mean we need to be enrolled in an institution of learning our entire lives, but we should have those around us who can provide new perspectives and insights to God's way of living. Personal, daily Bible reading, spiritual mentors and friends, and a community of those who trust Jesus and who live together as the church are key to whether or not our character will begin to look anything like the One who called us.

Who teaches you about the things of God? Who is actively involved in your life to teach you the character of God so that your character may someday look something like His? Are you a member of a group of Christ-followers who publicly live out their calling before others?

JESUS MODELED FOR THEM WHAT THIS NEW LIFE LOOKED LIKE. To teach without modeling is a signal the teacher is teaching someone else's material. To model what one teaches is proof the lesson comes from the teacher's life, not from a textbook. Jesus modeled what He taught His disciples. In our case study from Mark's story of Jesus (Mark 1:21–28), we observe Jesus' encounter with a man "with an unclean spirit." This is the next episode after Jesus called His disciples. When Jesus' new trainees joined Him in a local synagogue on the Sabbath, they heard Him teach. The people were amazed at His teaching because they said He taught with "authority, not as the teachers of the law," which meant His authority was unique in comparison to what they had heard before by others (v. 21). While Jesus taught, a man in the synagogue interrupted with a loud shout saying, "What do you want with us, Jesus of Nazareth? Have you come to destroy us? I know who you are—the Holy One of God!" (v. 24). Without hesitation, Jesus confronted the unclean spirit(s) and commanded them to leave the man. Like a scene from a special-effects horror film, the spirit "shook the man violently and came out of him with a shriek" (v. 26). Jesus demonstrated His authority over evil spirits as well as teaching with authority, unlike others before Him who had interpreted the Scriptures.

Jesus demonstrated that His message, "the kingdom of God is near," was authentic. He modeled the power of God's presence among the people and its superior strength over evil spirits. Jesus showed His new followers what He would invite them to do later. After Jesus left the synagogue, no one doubted His authoritative insights into Scripture and mastery over unclean spirits. Those who heard and saw Him that day marveled and asked, "What is this? A new teaching—and with authority! He even gives orders to evil spirits and they obey him" (v. 27). Jesus continued to model the "near kingdom of God" as He went to outcasts, touched lepers, stood against religious bigotry, and crossed social and religious barriers that separated people from God. He ultimately modeled the suffering, sacrificial love of God on the cross. Jesus' words were verified by His life.

The same is true in our lives. Our actions verify our words are true and that we can be trusted. Words are cheap, and the spin machine of our culture's media allows most any spoken word to be altered as needed. However, no one is fooled when a person says one thing but his or her actions tell another story. Hypocrisy is to wear the mask of appearances with the false assumption people will not be able to see the heart of the actor. True character is revealed when the mask is removed and the heart is exposed. To follow Jesus is to live mask-free before others so they may "see your good deeds and glorify your Father in heaven" (Matthew 5:16).

What have you done to model what you teach to others? Do your words match your actions? How have Jesus' teachings appeared in what you say and do?

JESUS EMPOWERED THEM. Let's go to the end of Jesus' ministry on earth and see how He empowered His disciples after He had called them, taught them, and modeled His teachings for them. Many students of the Bible know Jesus' commissioning words to His disciples recorded in Matthew 28:19–20. We know them as the Great Commission, and they apply to all followers of Jesus. While we know the heart of Jesus' sending message, we often overlook the content found in Matthew 28:18 where Jesus prefaced His commissioning by announcing, "All authority in heaven and on earth has been given to me." He *then* said, "Therefore go . . ." in verse 19. Jesus declared His authority prior to commissioning His followers. He sent them out under the authority of who He was as the Son of God. They were not to venture out under their own authority. Later, when His disciples encountered people or situations that required authority beyond them, they invoked the name of Jesus. (See Acts 3:1–10 for an example.)

At the end of verse 20, Jesus promised those He sent that He would be with them "always, to the very end of the age." Jesus empowered their disciple-making with His presence. How would He do that? He promised He would send "another advocate" in His final conversations with His disciples before His death (John 14:16). That advocate, the Holy Spirit, filled His disciples during the Festival of Pentecost in Jerusalem some 50 days after Jesus' death and resurrection (Acts 2:1–4). This same Holy Spirit would continue to fill, guide and empower those who trusted Jesus to be the Christ as they lived on mission with Him.

Jesus empowered his followers with the authority of His name and the power of His presence. After calling, teaching, and modeling His new way of life, Jesus did not leave His apprentices alone to figure things out on their own. Nor did He leave them to use the authority of their charisma, position, or intelligence to establish His spiritual kingdom on earth. We who follow Jesus' example will also share what authority we have in our relationship with Christ and our earthly authority with those we empower to live like Jesus. Further, we will be a presence in their lives they can depend upon and trust to be there when they need us.

Has anyone empowered you to develop under his or her leadership by sharing the authority of his or her name and/or supporting presence? How have you empowered someone by doing this for them? In what ways have you acted under the authority of Jesus' name and depended solely on the power of His presence for success?

A Pattern for Developing Character in Others

The Lord Jesus is our example for developing godly character in others. If we apply how He trained His disciples to how we may train others, we can see the pattern below.

Call them. Call those God has put in your life to join you in growing into the likeness of Jesus in your words and actions. Challenge them to change how they currently see and accept the world's ways in order to embrace the worldview and ways of God. They may not respond immediately, but when God births them into a vital relationship with Him, you can echo that call again.

Teach them. Developing godly character in another person means teaching the words and ways of Jesus. Be specific in your instructions about how they are to reflect Jesus' kingdom way of life in their own. Present the words of Jesus in ways they can understand, and apply those words to particular situations in their lives.

Model for them. Be an example of what God has called them to do and how you and others have taught them to do it. Let your behavior that is born out of a personal relationship with Jesus be the lesson they remember most. Take them along with you as Jesus did His disciples so they can experience the power of God in their lives.

Empower them. Share the authority you may have with the one you are developing so that they will not serve on their own. Promise your presence in times of need or uncertainty so they will not waver in their commitment to the call. Release them to call and empower others to join God in His eternal work on earth.

A Challenge for Our Day

- Jesus walked into the daily lives of the disciples to call them to a new way of life. When did Jesus enter your life and call you to join Him on mission?
- What are the major teachings of Jesus that have influenced you the most?

What will you do to increase your knowledge and understanding of what Jesus taught?

- Whose character have you begun to develop? How has this chapter helped you in that process? What one thing can you do this week to empower that person to demonstrate the character of Christ?

Further Study

Take time to dig a little deeper into how Jesus developed the character of His disciples.

- Read the major teachings of Jesus as recorded in Matthew's story of Jesus. Matthew 5–7, 10, 13, 18, and 24–25 contain most of Jesus' revealed teachings.

- Read one of the four Gospels, or stories, of Jesus in one sitting with the purpose of observing how He developed the character of those He encountered.

- Choose one of the disciples, such as Peter, James, or John, and observe how they changed as Jesus developed their character.

CHAPTER 11

Mary and Martha: Relationship Is the Key

e cannot have the character *of* Jesus until we spend time *with* Jesus. Just as athletes cannot reach their full potential without a coach so we, the followers of Jesus, must have personal contact with our Leader in order to understand how to live the life He has designed for us. The story of Jesus' friendship with Mary and Martha shows us the importance Jesus placed on *being with* Him over *doing things for* Him. It demonstrates how trusting Him is more than simply hearing His words— it's believing in Him. Jesus loved the two sisters and their brother, Lazarus, and He took time to mold their character as He reveals the power and presence of God before them.

Two Sisters, Two Characters

We meet the two sisters in the biblical narrative when Jesus came to a village, which we later discover is Bethany (Luke 10:38; John 11:18). This little town, about two miles east of Jerusalem, was the backdrop for two important events in Jesus' ministry: Jesus' raising of Lazarus from the dead (John 11) and the anointing of Jesus with expensive perfume just prior to His death (John 12:1–8). Mary and Martha played significant roles in each of the stories. John recorded these and other stories so that you would trust that "Jesus is the Christ, the Son of God, and that by believing you may have life in his name" (John 20:31).

Luke tells us that when Jesus entered the town, Martha received Him as a guest and began preparations to host Him. Her sister, Mary, on the other hand, sat at the feet of Jesus listening to His words (Luke 10:39). Martha's character reflected her respect for the traditions of her day and her commitment to doing what was expected of her when guests arrived. However, she became distracted from Jesus' teaching with the many services she had to perform, and she asked Jesus, "Lord, don't you care that my sister has left me to do the work by myself? Tell her to help me!" (10:40). Martha's heart told her the most important thing she could do for Jesus was to provide food and accommodations for Him. Hospitality shown to guests and family was highly valued in the Jewish culture, and Martha simply fulfilled her duty as a hostess to provide for Jesus and those who traveled with Him. Martha assumed her sister should aid in the preparation of the meal and arrangements.

Before we read Jesus' response to Martha's request, we must not condemn her for her actions or question them. Martha's training and sensitivity to do what was proper and expected drove her to the activity she created for herself. Her heart called her to care for her guest. Her sense of obligation insisted her sister should help if the load became too great.

How are you like Martha? What obligations—both social and religious—are high priorities in your life? How would you respond if other family members sat and talked to a guest while you worked in the kitchen to prepare the meal?

As we observe Jesus' response to Martha and His actions toward the two sisters in subsequent stories, we can learn how God develops our character through a personal, daily relationship with the Lord Jesus.

Jesus Challenges Our Expectations of Others

Jesus responded to Martha's request by identifying her misplaced expectations of her sister. He told her she had become "worried and upset about many things" (Luke 10:41). Her concern to feed and care for Jesus made her feel anxious and troubled. Her anxiousness reveals her inner struggle to do what was expected for guests, and her troubled feelings expose her angry heart toward her sister. Jesus contrasted Martha's harried actions with Mary's peaceful, resting spirit. He points out the one thing that is needed in her life will be learned not by activity, but by resting in Him. In doing so, He also condemns her attitude toward her sibling.

I (Gene) heard a speaker say, "Comparison is the great thief of joy." When we compare ourselves to others like Martha did with Mary, we limit our perspective to what they have or to what they are doing and miss the reality of God's presence in our lives. I cannot be joyful when comparing myself to others because there will always be someone with more money than I have, someone who is smarter than I am, and someone who is closer to God than I am. To compare is to rob ourselves of joy. It also shifts our focus from God to others which will bring immediate unrest to our hearts. It will lead to jealousy if someone is more successful or to pride if you feel you are more successful—both are listed in the sins of the flesh in Ephesians 5.

Make a list of concerns you have that cause anxiousness and a troubled spirit. Do you compare yourself with others? If so, take time to repent and allow God's peace to guard your heart and mind.

Jesus Values the Time We Spend at His Feet

Jesus told Martha, "Only one thing is needed," not all the things she scurried about to provide for Him (Luke 10:42). That one thing, Jesus noted, was what Mary had chosen: sitting at the feet of Jesus. He said Mary had chosen the thing that was "better" than Martha's choices, and He would not take that choice away from her sister by telling her to help Martha with the chores. We do not know Martha's response to Jesus, but we learn from Jesus' reply that the way to serve Him is to listen to His words rather than anxiously attending to His needs. Jesus valued time spent at His feet above time spent cleaning the floor where His feet would walk!

Our culture tends to value activity over sitting and listening, but if God develops character by our real-time relationship with Jesus, then our value system needs to change. Even activities that are socially or religiously required may not be "better" than time spent with Jesus listening and learning His Word. If we are to be like Jesus, we must spend time with Jesus, and He taught Martha that resting at His feet was more important than providing for His earthly needs. Mary chose the better of the two ways of serving Him that day.

What religious or social expectations take you away from time with Jesus in prayer, reading His Word, and simply spending time with Him? Spend time resting at Jesus' feet right now. Ask Him to show you any adjustments you need to make in order for your life and service to be exactly what He wants.

Jesus Guides Our Faith to Completion

The next time we meet the two sisters is when Jesus heard that His friend,

Lazarus, was ill (John 11:1). Jesus had experienced intense conflict with the religious leaders and had withdrawn to the place where John the Baptist "had been baptizing in the early days" (John 10:40). It was there that the word from Mary and Martha about their brother came to Him. When He learned of His friend's sickness, He revealed: "This sickness will not end in death. No, it is for God's glory so that God's Son may be glorified through it" (John 11:4). A greater purpose was at work in the illness and eventual death of His friend. We who trust Jesus must remember this truth as we face sickness and death in life.

When Jesus arrived in Bethany, Martha greeted Him and said, "Lord, if you had been here, my brother would not have died" (11:21). Jesus told her that her brother would "rise again," and she affirmed her trust in the resurrection—someday. Jesus then proclaimed one of the seven "I am" statements recorded by John (See John 6:51; 10:9; 10:11; 15:1 for other examples.). He revealed to His friend that she did not have to wait until the "last day" to see her brother raised from the dead because He was "the resurrection and the life" (11: 25). Jesus guided Martha's faith to completion and strengthened her character by revealing who He truly was. Mary said, like her sister, that if Jesus had been present when her brother was sick, he would not have died (11:32). The sisters declared their trust in Jesus, but their faith was not complete. Jesus patiently helped them see the fullness of who He was by coming to them at this moment. His timing was perfect— their faith was about to be extended exponentially.

Are there many areas in which our faith is incomplete? Do you trust Jesus fully with every experience in life no matter how extreme?

Jesus Empathizes with Our Grief

The shortest verse in the Bible is "Jesus wept" (John 11:35). This two-word sentence reveals the empathetic love God has for those who grieve. John tells us, "Jesus loved Martha and her sister and Lazarus" (11:5). John described Jesus' feelings when He saw Mary crying and those mourning who had come out to greet Him. Professional mourners and friends had joined the family in publicly grieving over the loss of Lazarus. While everyone fulfilled their obligation as mourners, they missed the fact Jesus was the "resurrection and the life" and that Lazarus had only "fallen asleep" (11:11). Jesus knew the rest of the story, but He wept with them. He wept for their lack of trust in Him. He wanted to give them hope in the face of death, but they only mourned. The Bible described Jesus as "deeply moved in spirit and troubled" (11:33). These are words that describe a disgusted or perturbed spirit, even one filled with anger. Jesus did not cry because they were crying. He loved His friends, and when He saw their lack of trust even in His presence, Jesus wept. "When will they believe that I am who I say that I am?" He might have thought.

This tiny verse reveals Jesus' empathetic heart for those He loved and for those who did not yet see Him for who He is. It is the compassionate response to those who do not trust Him for who He is. Jesus demonstrated the compassion of God that reaches out to those who mourn and modeled God's character that willingly enters the circumstances of people to share their grief and loss—no matter how misplaced that grief may be. Godly character is shown in empathetic emotions with those who suffer loss and a willingness to "mourn with those who mourn" (Romans 12:15). Biblical character weeps for those who do not trust Jesus fully but remains in the circumstance of loss to show Jesus' love.

When have you shown empathy for someone who has suffered loss? Did you take the opportunity to share your hope in Jesus?

Jesus Demonstrates His Power Through Resurrection

Jesus molded the character of Mary and Martha by publicly demonstrating that He was who He said He was. When Jesus had the mourners remove the stone from the tomb, practical-minded Martha pointed out that her brother had been in there four days and would reek with decay (John 11:39). Jesus reminded her of His words, "Did I not tell you that if you believed you would see the glory of God?" (11:40). Jesus humbly prayed to the Father and then called out "in a loud voice, 'Lazarus, come out!'"(11:43). The Bible says "the dead man came out" (11:44). Jesus truly was the resurrecting Messiah who showed His character and identity to those who watched that afternoon. Not only did Jesus teach about who He was, He continually demonstrated it in the middle of everyday experiences. Godly character acts out its true identity in daily circumstances.

The resurrection of Jesus was God's crowning work to reveal that Jesus is the Son of God and the Sent One of Israel. The raising of Lazarus from the dead was the "sign" that pointed to Jesus' own resurrection and the verification that His words, "I am the resurrection and the life," were trustworthy. Jesus' resurrection is the cornerstone of our faith without which our trust in Him would be "useless" (1 Corinthians 15:14).

Jesus' relationship with Mary and Martha shows us ways in which God molds our character. Time at Jesus' feet and trusting Him for who He says He is, no matter the circumstances, are fundamental for us to have the character of Christ. While we can become distracted by activity, Jesus calls us to sit at His feet and learn from Him how to be like Him so others may trust Him and experience His resurrection power in their lives.

A Challenge for Our Day

- Life's obligations and expectations can distract us from being with Jesus. You began a list earlier in this chapter of those things that distract you from time with Jesus. Continue that list now and then pray that God would reveal to you what adjustments you need to make in order to fully rest at His feet.

- Is your true confession that Jesus is "the resurrection and the life"? Is this true only for life after death, or does it impact your daily attitudes and actions?

- In what ways can you show the empathetic love of God to others today?

Further Study

Find Bethany on a map of the Holy Land. Look up several places in the Gospels where it is mentioned. Note what significant events took place there.

- Read John 12:1–11 to learn of one more shared experience Jesus had with the two sisters. Notice in this passage that Martha is still serving, and Mary is still at Jesus' feet. This time, however, Martha is serving peacefully. What a remarkable picture this gives us of Martha's character. Early in her knowledge of Jesus she served anxiously; now she is still serving, but peacefully.

- Look up the "I am" passages in the Gospel of John in order to discover the character of God revealed in Jesus, His Son.

CHARACTER THAT
MAKES A
DIFFERENCE

CHAPTER 12

The Unnamed Servant Girl: Character That Is Merciful

O ften, as we read a book like 2 Kings, we skim over the pages looking for the overall flow of history and key events that relate to the Israelite people. However, a closer look reveals valuable examples of both good and bad character. In some situations, we see how God deliberately developed character; while in others, we observe how people's character is revealed through the circumstances God allows in his or her life. In each case, the examples provide a challenge for any person who desires to follow after God.

Second Kings 5 is a familiar story recounting the way in which God chose to heal Naaman, the commander of the Syrian army, of leprosy. While the central issue for the chapter is that God reached out and impacted the life of a person outside of the people of Israel, a close look at the people involved in the story provides valuable truths concerning character for our day.

Take a moment to read the narrative story of Naaman in 2 Kings 5. Pay close attention to the people involved: Naaman, the young girl, the two kings, Elisha, the servant of Naaman, and Gehazi. A careful look at this passage provides many examples of character from the prophet Elisha, who does not accept any gifts from Naaman (in order to declare that it was God who healed the general), to the example of Naaman whose pride is so great that he is willing to walk away from the opportunity for healing. For our case study we want to focus on one often overlooked but vital person to the outcome of the story—the servant girl.

John Hunter, a wonderful servant of the Lord and Christian author, often shared a message centered on the picture of door hinges. Living in England, he would point out the enormous doors on the cathedrals and classical buildings and then note that regardless of the size, weight, or magnificence of the doors, they all swung on small, and often unnoticed, hinges. In this account we could certainly call Naaman and Elisha the large doors. The wonderful outcome, however, would not have occurred without the "hinges" of the story, that is, the characters who seem to be secondary to the story.

The original audience of the text would most likely not identify with Naaman or the great prophet Elisha, and especially not with the kings, but rather with the unnamed girl as well as the servants (most likely the servant of Naaman). Let's examine the role the young girl played in the story. Did you recall the young girl's name in the story? Her name was not even given, but how much of the story would have taken place if she was not included? How much of the account is dependent on her character and the outcome it would produce? She is not forced to respond the way she does in verses 2–3, but rather she makes a choice to get involved in the drama of Naaman's leprosy. Her actions reveal character (especially for her young age) that would have been recognized by the original audience of the story and serves as a challenge to all readers of the text. We may not always see ourselves as the key leader determining the outcome of an event or decision at our workplace or home but, like the young girl, the activity of God is tied to our attitudes and actions.

A Closer Look into the Text

The account does not provide much information about the young girl on the surface; however, we can draw quite a lot from the story.

First, she is described as a young girl. This fact alone serves as a challenge to adult readers of the text. We like to think that we grow in our faith in the Lord as we get older. After all, we have walked with God through life's experiences longer and have gained more wisdom over the years. But what we see in the text is a young girl who, even in the face of the tragedy of being taken captive, reveals remarkable character. The amount of time she has spent serving in her captor's house is not mentioned, but it does not appear that there is much distance between the raids and her declaration concerning the prophet in Israel.

Second, the young girl has gone through a ruthless experience as Naaman has led his army to raid her village. The text does not elaborate on the raid, but raids like this could be very brutal. Verse 2 of the chapter describes Naaman as leading multiple raids with bands of men through the Israelite country in what must have been a regular exercise to kill, destroy, and carry off possessions and people. At this point, let's think through the events of this raid and the impact it would have on this young girl. As a father, I can't imagine allowing my daughters to be taken captive. In fact, like most parents, I would lay down my life trying to prevent someone from taking my children away from me to make them slaves in a foreign land. It is safe to assume that this girl's family would have felt the same way. Most likely those in her family who were of fighting age had been killed and the younger siblings taken captive.

Third, she has been taken from her homeland and is now serving as a slave in the home of the man who was responsible for raiding her village, possibly killing her family, and carting her off to a foreign land. So, how would you be doing at this point? Remembering that Naaman is the commander of the hated enemy who has been raiding Israel, what do you think the response would be of the original audience? Do you think the average Israelite would have compassion on Naaman and his leprosy? It is in this moment we begin to see the challenge that the text presents through this young girl. How would you act if you had to serve in the house of the man who raided your town, killed your family and took you into slavery? And even more important, how would you "feel" about God and your relationship with Him?

Character Revealed in Faith and Confidence in the Lord

I have to admit that if I were in this girl's situation I am not sure how much mercy or compassion would be in my heart toward Naaman. I might be thinking that this slow and painful leprosy was very fitting for the man who had taken me captive. Would I really want to see God show mercy to my enemy or, would I have been praying for his ruin? We don't see any of these thoughts in the text. The opening verses state that God had been the One who had given Naaman his victories, and clearly God was taking the initiative to transform the general's life. So, this compassion shown by the young girl may have been a result of God using her to unfold His plan. *She seems to show compassion for a man who had none for her*, and then she reveals her faith and confidence in the Lord and His prophet. "She said to her mistress, 'If only my master would see the prophet who is in Samaria! He would cure him of his leprosy" (2 Kings 5:3).

She may have been a captive outside of her homeland, but she was an Israelite who knew her God and His prophet. Both Elisha and his predecessor Elijah were known as champions for God and men *on whom the spirit of the Lord rested.* We see a bold trust in God here. She not only knows that Elisha serves God, but is certain that if Naaman could meet with the prophet, he would find healing. Rather than stay quiet, she reveals her confidence in the God of Israel by taking the next step and sharing this confidence in God with her mistress, Naaman's wife. Again, the text does not give us all the details, but her trust in Elisha and the God he served must have been convincing since the commander of the Syrian army went and told his king "what the girl from Israel had said" (v. 4). The girl's confidence must have been impressive for the king immediately to send Naaman with an official letter, ten talents of silver, 6,000 shekels of gold, and ten changes of clothing (v. 5). Some might want to dismiss the girl and say, "Well, Naaman had leprosy; of course he would be willing to try anything at this point." But the text reveals Naaman as a very proud man, who was even willing to walk away from this healing because he did not like the way he was treated by Elisha (v. 11).

The Impact of Character

GOD CAN USE PEOPLE WHO HAVE A CONFIDENT TRUST IN HIM. This young girl had experienced great trauma in her life and yet revealed an unwavering trust in God. Rather than questioning God or focusing on her circumstances, she makes a clear declaration that the prophet in Israel could take care of Naaman's leprosy. This assertion about Elisha was not in the man himself. As an Israelite girl she would have a clear understanding that the prophet was a representative of and empowered by the God of Israel. She had not lost faith in God due to her captivity. She does not question the power of her God because He has allowed her to be taken. This declaration also indicates that she did not hold bitterness toward God for her circumstances. At this young age, this girl showed character that serves as a challenge for our day when so many people determine their trust and faith in God based on their personal circumstances or experiences.

GOD CAN USE PEOPLE WHO PUT THEIR PERSONAL TRAGEDIES ASIDE
AND ARE MERCIFUL TOWARD OTHERS. Probably the most challenging
revelation about this young girl's character is the fact that she shows
compassion to a man who was responsible for her pain. Syria was a hated
enemy of Israel and the Books of 1 and 2 Kings indicate constant warfare
between the two nations. This was not the first or presumably last raid that
Naaman would conduct as commander of the Syrian king's army. Yet, the
young girl sees the general's leprosy and takes the initiative to speak to his
wife about how he can be healed. There is no indication that the girl was
aware of God's plans for Naaman. She does not appear to know that the
success of Naaman had come from God. The text indicates that Naaman
himself did not attribute his success to God or even acknowledge the God of
Israel until he was healed later in the story. She simply showed compassion
in a rarely seen manner.

Character That Makes a Difference

The story of Naaman is a critical account for the message of the Old
Testament. Along with the Book of Jonah, the account teaches that God was
actively seeking out and impacting people outside of the nation of Israel.
Yet, one of the key figures in this account goes without a name. She is simply
"a young girl." But how much of this story hinges on her character? There
are only three verses in the story that mention the young girl, but her faith
in God and mercy toward her enemy are essential for Naaman to encounter
God. She was certainly a key part of this narrative and could be described
as a small "hinge" that turned a very large door!

A Challenge for Our Day

- How much of your faith in God is dependent upon your personal circumstances? While you most likely are not facing a situation like this young girl, how confident are you in your Lord when you are facing difficulties?

- How much are you willing to lay aside so that God can bring healing to those who have wronged you or those close to you? Are you merciful? Do you find yourself hoping for God's judgment on your enemies or praying for God's transformation of your enemies?

- When you are in the middle of circumstances that seem out of control or that you have no impact upon, are you living with an expectation that to remain faithful to God creates an opportunity for God to use you in mighty ways?

Further Study

We have just touched the surface of a passage that has many other wonderful teachings on character. For future study:

- You could also compare the difference in character of the servant of Naaman to the servant of Elisha. You would think that the one who served the prophet of the Lord would know the importance of selflessness better than the one who served Naaman.

- Compare the way in which the two kings conduct themselves. Should there be a difference in a king who does not worship God and one who is leading the people of God?

- Study the character of Elisha. Can you see how and why he was determined not to take credit for God's activity in the story?

CHAPTER 13

Hannah: Character That Trusts God

ow often have you found yourself attempting to bargain with God in the midst of a difficult or troubling situation? I think most of us would have to admit that there have been times that we pleaded with God to resolve a hurtful or devastating situation in return for our promised commitment to serve or "do a better job" following Him. How well did you do keeping your promised commitment to God once the problem was solved or the situation turned around? Sometimes we can forget a Scripture like Ecclesiastes 5:1–7 warns us not to make hasty vows to God. But what does it say about our character (our intimate fellowship with God) that we can so quickly go back on promised actions toward God once we are no longer under pressure? There is a wonderful, but very challenging, example from the Old Testament of a woman who, in the middle of great distress, made a significant commitment to God for His deliverance. God does hear her prayer and deliver her, and she in turn honors her vow. Her story does not end with her changed circumstances but, through the honoring of her vow, God was able to bless the entire nation of Israel and ultimately all those who would read her story in the Bible.

Often when reading the great stories of the Bible, we can overlook the fact that so many of the heroes of the faith were shaped by very ordinary people and events. Throughout our study we hope it has become very clear that the large majority of the people of the Bible were very ordinary, but through their trust and fellowship with God, they were united with an extraordinary God who used them to accomplish His eternal purpose. Certainly Samuel is one of the key figures of the Old Testament, the only person to hold all three offices of judge, priest, and prophet. He is the transitional figure that God used to move the people of God from the period of the Judges to the period of the monarchy. However, the two-volume work titled after this great figure (1 and 2 Samuel) does not begin with his story, but rather the story of his mother Hannah. We don't know much about Hannah. In fact, the opening chapter of First Samuel does not begin with her background but with her husband Elkanah and his impressive pedigree (1 Samuel 1:1). For the story of Hannah, her background is not important. What is important is the example of her commitment as she drew near to God in the midst of her distress, found hope and settled her faith in the Lord, and followed through on her vow to give her son to the Lord.

READ 1 SAMUEL 1:1 TO 2:11.

A Closer Look at the Text

After reading the text, it becomes clear that there are some cultural issues that impact the life of Hannah that we do not face today. First, she is married to a man who has two wives. During this period in Israel's early history, it was acceptable and common for men to have multiple wives, but this practice was put aside by the end of the Old Testament and certainly is unacceptable in the New Testament church. This practice of multiple wives often brought strife, jealousy, and competition between the wives and their children. A second cultural issue that Hannah faced was the role of women and the importance of bearing children. In a male-dominated society, it was considered the woman's fault if a couple could not have children. Because children were considered a blessing from God, a woman who could not have children was considered to have been in disfavor with God.

Hannah is introduced while in great distress as Peninnah (Hannah's rival wife) "kept provoking her in order to irritate her." We don't get a good impression of Peninnah as the text indicates that this was a continual practice to harass Hannah that had gone on for years (1 Samuel 1:7). The trip they had taken for this yearly worship and sacrifice would have included times of feasts and family meals together. We can assume that not only was Hannah overcome with grief for her situation, but she did not want to take part in the family celebration and meals where Peninnah and her children were honored and took part in the sacrifices (1:4). We begin to catch a picture of her inner struggle in verse 10: "In bitterness of soul Hannah wept much and prayed to the Lord."

In the midst of her anguish we are reminded through the text that her barrenness was not simply a biological problem, but that "the Lord had closed her womb" (v. 6). The text does not tell us why God had chosen to close her womb, but it seems that this source of grief and the harassment from Peninnah had driven Hannah to become an exceptional woman of faith in God. It served to develop character—a character that would eventually impact the entire nation. The description of Hannah places her as one of the most remarkable women in the entire Old Testament, and her prayer in chapter 2 is one of the longest prayers recorded in the Hebrew Scriptures. Many believe it is the prayer that Mary the mother of Jesus draws upon for her own praise to God in the Gospels.

Hannah's character begins to show in how she responds to her grief and harassment. She is not simply sad or angry, but the text uses the term "bitterness of soul." This is a phrase that was used in the Scriptures to describe great pain. Naomi used these words when she had lost her husband and two sons and felt that God had afflicted her (Ruth 1:13, 20). Job used the same words as he expressed his anguish over his situation (Job 3:20). Yet, Hannah understands that there is only One to whom she can bring her complaint (1:16). This is a key practice that Hannah displays here as she turns to the Lord. Clearly her husband loved her, but by his response in 1:8 he did not understand her grief, nor had he dealt with the continual harassment of his other wife.

The prayer must have continued for a lengthy period as she "was pouring out [her] soul before the Lord" (1:15). However, we are only told that she made a vow that should God give her a son, she would give this son back to the Lord. The intensity of her complaint to God was great enough that Eli mistook her for intoxicated and sought to remove her from the place of worship. How intense was her petition or complaint to God? All of the grief from the years of Peninah's mocking, coupled with the shame from her culture, were wrapped up in this experience as she poured out her heart to God. She quickly defends herself from Eli's accusation of being intoxicated, stating that she is not a wicked woman, but is calling upon her God and seeking His intervention and deliverance from her circumstances.

There is a dramatic change in the countenance of Hannah once Eli realizes she is making a petition to God, and He in turn announces a blessing upon Hannah stating that God would grant her request. Based on the first four chapters of First Samuel, it is clear that the priest Eli did not walk with or completely honor God. Nevertheless, he understood that Hannah was indeed sober and pouring her heart out to God. He therefore told her to go in peace and proclaimed that God would grant her request. Notice the transformation that takes place at the end of verse 18. What happened to Hannah that she could go from being described as in "bitterness of soul" to "the woman [who] went her way and ate and her face was no longer sad" (1:18 ESV)? She had spent time with God making her request and presenting her vow to God for His help. There was a confident faith, and she believed the words of Eli that God had heard her request. After years of this torment, she was certain her request had been heard and answered. Therefore, she ate, took part in the festivals, then returned home. How confident are you when you pour your heart out to God that He has heard and will be bringing the answer or deliverance? There was no indication at this point that she would have a child except for her confidence that God had heard her vow; that was enough for Hannah.

It is important to remember that her request was not simply that she would receive a son, but it was tied to her vow that she would give this son back to the Lord (1:11). We would suggest that this was always a part of Hannah's understanding and that she had not simply made a careless vow to God in a time of distress. For many of us who have made quick promises or attempted to bargain with God, the remainder of chapter 1 is very challenging. Yet, Hannah does not show any indication that she wavered on her vow with God. God had granted her request and now she would fulfill her part. "I prayed for this child, and the Lord has granted me what I asked of him. So now I give him to the LORD. For his whole life he shall be given over to the LORD. And he worshiped the Lord there" (1 Samuel 1:27–28). As parents it is hard to imagine the commitment exhibited here by Hannah. However, any sense of loss on her part (which is not described in the text) was far outweighed by the blessing this son was to be for the nation of Israel.

Character Revealed in Fulfilling Her Vows

As you read through and think about this story of Hannah, do you sense her dedication of heart and her trust in God? The strong sense of pain in her heart had not grown into bitterness toward God. After all, the text tells us that it was God who had closed her womb so that she could not have children. She understands that there is only one place to take her request. But for Hannah and this account, her fulfillment of her vow to God in verses 1:21–28 shows remarkable character of heart. She is thankful to God, knowing that He alone is the source of her blessing. Yet, how would you respond if you were in her place? First there is the bond that she would have as a mother. She has prayed and hoped for this child for so long, and now at such a young age, she was taking him to Shiloh to leave him with the priest. There is a confidence that she must fulfill her vow, but there is also a deep trust and confidence that her son will be safely cared for and raised apart from her. Thinking through the first chapters of 1 Samuel, how many of us would be confident to leave our longed-for son in the care of Eli? He certainly did not do well with his own sons, based on Scriptures like 2:12–17 and 2:22–25. The people of Israel knew of the sons' corruption. However, Hannah had not entrusted her son simply to Eli, but had given him to the Lord in whom she had a confident faith. She understood that God's fulfillment of her request was not unrelated to her vow to give her son back to God. God would take care of her son. It is at this point we see the larger purposes of God as He begins to unfold His plan to "raise up for myself a faithful priest, who will do according to what is in my heart and mind" (1 Samuel 2:35).

How would you respond as you left your son in Shiloh? Chapter 2 gives us a clear picture of her heart toward God. She has just dedicated her son and her heart was rejoicing in the Lord (2:1). She is thankful that her enemies have been silenced by the Lord's actions. Hannah's dignity and self-worth have been restored; however her prayer quickly moves to wholehearted praise of God as the One who judges all and rewards those who seek Him. Certainly Hannah's life was a testimony to this fact.

The Impact of Character

THERE MAY BE TIMES WHEN GOD BRINGS HARDSHIP INTO OUR LIVES TO DEVELOP OUR DEPENDENCE ON HIM. For Hannah, the years of torment from the rival wife and the personal struggle of barrenness brought hardship and deep sorrow. Rather than turning away from God in frustration, she sought God for His deliverance with greater intensity. From her perspective the early years of her life were painful. However, from the larger perspective, God was intending to bless an entire nation through her. One wonders if she would have been willing to "lend" her son to the Lord had she not struggled through many years of hardship first. While we certainly don't desire to learn life's lessons and have our character built through pain, we must be open to see troubling times as opportunities to develop a greater dependence on God.

GOD USES PEOPLE WHO KEEP THEIR VOWS TO HIM. Hannah had no idea that keeping her vow to God would become a blessing to her entire nation. She simply understood that her God had answered her prayer to deliver her from her rival and redeem her from dishonor within her community. What she expresses as a joyous act of obedience brought her into the larger context of God's activity. God had been planning to remove Eli and his sons for their unfaithfulness and replace them with a faithful priest who would hear from Him and obey. This process would start with the faithful sacrifice of a mother who began a heritage of faith and set an example for Samuel as well as all who would read her story.

Character That Makes a Difference

The story of Hannah provides one of the greatest examples of fulfilling a vow to God in the Bible. We cannot overlook the cost of Hannah's act of obedience as she gave up her long-hoped-for son. (We are told in 2:21 that God graciously rewarded her sacrifice by giving her five more children.) However, her loss of a son to the work of God was huge gain for the people of God. Through her faith and trust to lend her son to God, God was able to raise up a faithful priest who would bring religious stability to the people as well as serve as God's instrument to anoint his servant David. It is important to realize that she was an ordinary woman who chose to turn to God and allow Him to work through her to bless her entire nation.

A Challenge for Our Day

- Where do you typically turn in time of great distress? Do you turn inward or to others for help? Have you determined that regardless of your circumstances you will stay before the Lord and pour your heart out to Him until you believe that He has heard you and will bring about a solution to your problem?
- Have you been quick to attempt to bargain with God or to make commitments to Him in order to be delivered from difficult times? Were you faithful to fulfill all of your vows to God that were made in times of crisis? If not, will you take time to repent and ask God to help you fulfill your vows to Him so that He can use your life as a blessing to others?
- Have you been selfish with the blessings and gifts of God? Are you prepared to give back to the Lord all the blessings that He has given to you so that your life can serve as an example and instrument for His purposes?

Further Study

There are many examples of those who have determined to keep vows or commitments to obey and honor God at great personal risk or cost. Take time to study the following examples and see how God can challenge your personal relationship with God.

- Read Daniel 1. Take note of Daniel and his companions' concern not to violate God's requirements for purity. To what lengths are you willing to go to make sure you remain undefiled in our world?
- Read Acts chapters 21–23. Paul understood that God had called him to go to Jerusalem. However, at every step of his journey well-meaning Christians tried to convince him not to go for fear of his life. Take time to study Paul's determination to honor God even when he knew he faced certain danger.

CHAPTER 14

Joseph: Character That Preserves Life

H ow quick are you to obey or follow after God when He gives you direction or reveals His plans to you? You may be wondering, how do I really know when He is speaking in the first place? We won't take time to argue the biblical points concerning knowing when God is speaking or if He has a specific will or plan for my life at this time. If you struggle with these issues, we would suggest the helpful books titled *Experiencing God: Knowing and Doing the Will of God* and *Called and Accountable* to help bring clarity. For us, it is clear that God speaks to His people in the Bible and the testimony of Scripture and Christian history reveal that God's people not only experience God speaking, but also understand what He is saying. But, how do you respond when God speaks to you? Does a sense of urgency come over you when God speaks? It has been said often that one of the issues of American Christianity is that we have adapted our governmental beliefs into the Christian life and treat the Kingdom of God as more of a democracy than a kingdom. When God speaks to us, we want to think about the merits of acting on His Word or we want to discuss it and give our input. But godly character does not enter into a "merits" discussion of God's speaking. Character that is born out of the love of and for God (John 14:23–24) simply obeys immediately, for this kind of character realizes the importance of God's timing when He speaks.

Often when the name Joseph comes up in Bible study settings, people automatically assume this is a reference to the Old Testament stories of Genesis. However, the New Testament opens with a very impressive story of a man named Joseph who played an important role in the life of Jesus. He is often overlooked for his role in the gospel story, but the Book of Matthew provides an important account of Joseph's character that was critical in protecting and preserving the lives of Mary and Jesus.

Joseph is called a "righteous," "up-right," or "just man" depending on the translation. This is not to mean that he was a perfect man, but Matthew uses this term to describe someone who is law-abiding and upright in character, someone who had a heart to honor and obey God and His commandments. We will see Joseph's character on display through the beginning chapters of Matthew. First, we will see his character as he deals with the issue of Mary's pregnancy, but what is really impressive and a challenge for our day is the way in which he immediately obeys God at each stage of the story. Joseph is not given much detail through God's direction but he immediately responds, and it is this reaction—or pattern of obedience—that protects his wife and the baby Jesus.

A Closer Look at the Text

As stated above, Joseph is described as a just or righteous man. The Bible does not go into detail describing why he is designated this way or why he is chosen for the important task of watch-care over Mary and Jesus. However, it becomes very clear in the opening chapters why God could trust Joseph with such a significant role in the early life of our Lord. As you read the text, be careful to think through what a just man looks like in this story. In particular, watch to see how Joseph responds each time God's messenger speaks to him. How important was it that he respond in the manner he did, and how did his character impact his family?

READ MATTHEW 1:18 TO 2:23.

You may have noticed that there are four occasions in this brief story where Joseph is either divinely warned or spoken to by an angel in a dream. Each one of these instances reveals the man's character as he responds to the activity of God. When we first hear of Joseph in chapter 1, he has just found out his "wife-to-be" was pregnant. It was the custom for a woman who was promised to a man to stay with her family for a year. This was regarded as the first stage of marriage. After this year the woman would move to the man's home where they would establish the marriage. It appears that Mary and Joseph were in this first stage of their marriage. Mary's pregnancy was extremely serious for her day since she could be considered an adulteress by Jewish law and receive the most severe of punishments—death by stoning (Deuteronomy 22).

We meet Joseph as he is contemplating what to do with Mary. We get a glimpse into his character as his desire is not to make Mary a public example and subject her to ridicule and possible punishment (1:19). There is no indication that he wanted revenge or to have her dealt with according to the law. This "just" man shows mercy to Mary. He had not decided what he was going to do at the time the angel came to him, assured him that Mary had not committed adultery, and instructed him to take Mary as his wife. The "just" or righteous response to the angel: "Joseph . . . did what the angel of the Lord had commanded him." Again, Matthew's description of Joseph as one who is righteous—not perfect—but faithful to the commands of the Lord is evidenced in his immediate obedience (1:24).

The story of Joseph is picked up in Matthew 2:13, after the departure of the wise men. Again, Joseph is warned in a dream. This time the angel warns him to flee because Herod the Great is going to be seeking to kill

Jesus (2:13). Very few details are provided and Joseph is warned to keep his family in Egypt until he is instructed to return. The "just" man responds: "so he got up . . . and left for Egypt." What a track record! He does not wait and wonder what he should do. He does not spend the day getting ready; rather, the text states as soon as he awoke, he got up, gathered his wife and child, and headed to Egypt. The text does not tell us how much time elapsed between Joseph's departure and Herod's massacre (2:16–18), but it seems to indicate some sense of urgency for the family to depart quickly. When God's message gets through to you do you have this same sense of urgency? While we may not have a ruling despot trying to kill our family, can God warn us of potential danger that can bring spiritual death to one of our children, a relationship, our employment, or even our marriage? What does your immediate response to God's direction reveal about your character?

The text does not tell us how long Joseph kept his family in Egypt, but once Herod was dead, the angel of the Lord announced to Joseph that it was safe to return (2:20). We don't know what he was doing while away from his homeland. It is safe to assume that the family was well provided for, based on the treasures or gifts they had received from the wise men (2:11). Joseph must have been content to trust that he was to stay in Egypt until further notice from God. He simply trusted God to direct his path and protect his family. When he does receive instruction, we see once again how a person of upright character responds: "So he got up, took the child and his mother and went to the land of Israel" (2:21).

In the process of heading home, Joseph discovers that Archelaus was ruling over Judah rather than his father Herod. Archelaus was known as a cruel ruler. In fact, the leaders in Rome quickly recognized his inability to rule and removed him in A.D. 6. Joseph was afraid that his family might be in danger living under this cruel ruler. Certainly, if Archelaus was anything like his father, Joseph's fears were well-founded. In the midst of his fear, God confirms Joseph's concerns and directs him to change his destination northward to the region of Galilee. There is no discussion of what transpired in the dream, but we do know that God warned him and Joseph changed directions (2:23).

Character Revealed in Immediate Obedience

When you read this account, it is clear that God was working out His plan of salvation for mankind through the lives of Mary, Joseph, and Jesus. Did you catch the continued emphasis throughout the passage showing how each event was predicted or was the fulfillment of Scripture (see vv. 1:22; 2:5; 2:17; and 2:23)? Clearly God was protecting and providing for Jesus during His infancy. God chose godly parents to be honored with His Son, God provided financial support for the stay in Egypt through the wise men, and God provided warnings to Joseph at the appropriate times to protect the life of Jesus. We would argue that part of this provision was provided in an earthly father who had a righteous character. We see this character exhibited in his desire to show mercy to Mary when it appeared she had shamed both of them by getting pregnant before marriage. Rather than take offence at the breach of trust and seeming lack of morals of his bride-to-be, he was pondering how to deal best with the manner in a kind way. Remember this was before the angel had informed Joseph of the nature of Mary's pregnancy.

The challenge from this account of Joseph really comes with his immediate response to the activity of God. We believe it was this quality of character that allowed him to be used in such a special way in the plan of God. Remember that Joseph is recorded to be a carpenter (Matthew 13:55).

He is not a great religious leader, a priest, or a teacher of the Scripture, but a skilled laborer who had a habit of honoring God and His Law. What do you look for when selecting a person to hold or have a significant role in the things of God? When a leadership position is vacant and the church or Christian organization is looking for someone who will be faithful to hear from God and obey the ways of God, what do you look for? Do we place skills over character, wealth over faithfulness, position and influence over integrity? We are not suggesting that skill and background are not important, but what better thing could be said about people than "when God spoke to them, he or she wants to obey immediately." Joseph was not responsible to figure out how to protect his family; he was simply responsible to obey quickly when God brought warning. How do you respond when God speaks to you? You may not have God speaking through angels during your dreams, but you will have God speaking to you. In reality, you have a much greater opportunity for God to speak to you as a Christian. One of the Trinity, the Holy Spirit, has been given to you and assigned by God the Father to guide you. John's Gospel tells us that the Holy Spirit will abide with you forever, that He dwells with you and will be in you (John 14:16–17). If you take a quick look at all the New Testament tells us concerning the role the Father has given the Holy Spirit in our lives, we can have confidence that God will be directing us.

What is your track record of obedience? What does your response time to God's voice reveal about your character? What kind of adjustments are you willing to make based on God's leading? As a result of a simple message from God in his dreams, Joseph uprooted his family and left his country. Was it worth it? What would it have cost him and his family if he had been a man of lesser character? What could have happened if he had stopped to debate with God or even other family members the issues or merits of a move to Egypt?

The Impact of Character

GOD USES THE PERSON WHOSE IMMEDIATE RESPONSE TO HIS DIRECTION IS TO OBEY. With all the studies on the life and character of Mary, Joseph is often overlooked. However, God would not just choose Joseph out of happenstance. This "just" man was one who obeyed God. Obedience is often a word avoided in our culture. We prefer to "discuss" our options with God at times. However, the New Testament is very clear that every Christian has entered into a master-servant relationship, and the servant by the very nature of the relationship must obey. We must also remember that the obedience is not done through a harsh system of rewards and punishments, but out of the overflow of a love relationship (John 14:21). Out of a love for God, Joseph immediately responded to the words of God and, in turn, God was able to invite Joseph into one of the greatest activities of human history. What would God be able to invite you to be involved with, based on your immediate reactions to His will and purposes?

WHEN GOD GIVES US DIRECTION, WE NEED TO RECOGNIZE THAT OUR RESPONSE (OBEDIENCE) CAN HAVE SIGNIFICANT IMPACT ON THOSE AROUND US. For Joseph, he must have realized that his actions had enormous consequences. He was caring for his wife as well as the Son of God. Each time he arose early and acted in obedience, there were immediate consequences for his family and ultimately mankind. How have you viewed your actions or responses to God's activity? While you may not feel that your actions will impact others, we do not live independent lives as Christians. I assume that most people reading these words do not relate to people who face death from tyrannical rulers. However, our actions will impact people who are making decisions that may lead to spiritual life or death. Are there people who would seek to destroy your children's ideas at school or work? What if God woke you up in the middle of the night to warn you of a relationship that could devastate the life of one of your children or a close friend? How quickly would you respond to God's direction and adjust your life for the sake of others?

A Challenge for Our Day

- How would God describe your character based on your past responses to His direction? Are you someone who quickly and thoroughly honors God's direction when He speaks to you through reading your Bible, in prayer, during a sermon, or other means? Remember that Joseph was not a perfect man but one who had a heart to honor God and obey His commands.
- Are you careful to watch the way you live out your relationship with God? Are you aware of how your obedience or disobedience impacts others around you? When God gives you direction, do you step back and look at the big picture rather than simply how it directly impacts your personal life?

Further Study

Read Hebrews 11, a chapter that includes many stories of men and women who had a heart to trust and obey God, They heard God's voice—listened to God—and obeyed with very little direction. In addition, their obedience impacted those around them and people for generations to come.

CHAPTER 15

Barnabas:
Character That Comes
Alongside Others

is real name was Joseph, but his friends called him Barnabas. His nickname meant "son of encouragement," and it is easy to see how he gained such a reputation. We first meet Barnabas in the Book of Acts after he sold some family land and placed the proceeds at the feet of the apostles in order to meet the needs of others who were part of the newly formed church (Acts 4:36). This was no small feat since property was then, as it is now, a treasured commodity and often handed down from generation to generation. His sacrificial gift aided others who had trusted Jesus and had joined this movement of the Holy Spirit.

"Encouragement" in the original language carried the flavor of "to come alongside" someone. Joseph gained the reputation of coming alongside others to encourage or help them. His gift of the proceeds of the land sale encouraged the leaders of the church and those who were in need of care in a society, which had pushed them to the margins of life. We will see that his nickname also matched his desire to come alongside a relative who had been branded a failure. He encouraged this younger man (John Mark) in order to restore him to a place of honor and service.

Barnabas's honest act of charity stands in stark relief to the gift of Ananias and Sapphira in the following chapter of Acts. This couple wanted the reputation of being generous to people without the cost. Luke tells us that they sold personal property like Joseph, but rather than give the entire amount to the leaders, Ananias—with the full knowledge of his wife—kept some for himself. He, however, gave the appearance he had given all the proceeds of the sale to the church. Led by the Holy Spirit, Peter exposed their hypocrisy, and they both suffered a sudden death (Acts 5:1–10). God would not allow hypocrisy to infect the church. The character of God's people was far more important than what was in the bank.

The opposite of integrity is hypocrisy, and in matters of character hypocrisy is the deathblow to a person's reputation and his or her present walk with God. Barnabas, with pure motives and honest actions, displayed character with integrity, which is a singleness of heart for the ways of God. Jesus called it "pure in heart" in Matthew 5:8. Integrity is an undivided heart in the same way an integer is indivisible—without fractions cluttering the problem. Ananias and Sapphira gave the appearance—wore masks of pure hearts they did not have—of being generous while on the inside they had selfish hearts. Ananias may have been the perpetrator, but Sapphira was an accomplice and, like an accomplice to a crime, both were found guilty in the court of God's justice.

Godly character is based upon a pure heart. Jesus rebuked the religious leaders of his day for giving the appearance of pure hearts while harboring sinful motives. Jesus said, for example,

Woe to you, teachers of the law and Pharisees, you hypocrites! You are like whitewashed tombs, which look beautiful on the outside but on the inside are full of the bones of the dead and everything unclean.
—MATTHEW 23:27

Religion and religious activity are susceptible to playacting because the act of faith is designed to be a reflection of the heart and one's relationship with God. However, we have all learned to act religiously while our motives in no way resemble the heart of God. This is why the prophets told the people, "Behold, to obey is better than sacrifice, and to heed than the fat of rams" (1 Samuel 15:22 NASB). Even God's prescribed sacrifices were null and void if worshippers did not live out what God had told them to do. A pure heart means a heart that is undivided—a heart that is fully submitted to the purposes and ways of God.

CHARACTER THAT MAKES A DIFFERENCE DISPLAYS A HEART OF INTEGRITY AND GENEROSITY. Barnabas had a generous heart. He also was a man of integrity when compared to the generosity of Ananias and Sapphira. His character reflected the giving nature of the heart of God. His knowledge of God's Word as a faithful member of Israel's tribe of Levi and his fullness of the Holy Spirit as a member of Christ's church gave him a generous heart like the One who gave Himself for the forgiveness of our sins. To be known as a "person of encouragement" is a nickname followers of Jesus should wear today as we share the resources God gives us in order to bless others.

Integrity is still the foundation for generosity in the church today. Why do you give to your local church or nonprofit? Is it simply for the tax break? Or, are you genuinely giving as an act of charity for those in need? Would you give if there was no governmental support for your giving? Do you give as Jesus said, "But when you give to the needy, do not let your left hand know what your right hand is doing"? (Matthew 6:3 TNIV).

Barnabas may be best known in biblical history for bringing Saul of Tarsus, better known as the Apostle Paul, into the church. Saul, a Pharisee and enemy of the church, met the risen Lord while on the road to Damascus. He was traveling to Damascus in order to arrest members of the new sect who trusted Jesus was the Messiah (Acts 9). As you would guess, those early followers were a bit skeptical of his sincerity as a new disciple of Jesus.

Would you welcome a former KGB agent into your home church if you were a Russian Christian during the 70-year reign of Communism? When this new convert showed up in Jerusalem to meet the apostles, it was Barnabas who came alongside him and vouched for his authentic faith. Barnabas told the assembly of Saul's powerful preaching in Damascus immediately after his conversion. The son of encouragement said they could trust the former persecutor to be who he said he was, and because of Barnabas' character they believed his witness (Acts 9:27–28). As far as the biblical record goes, we do not hear of any other doubts about Paul being a genuine follower of Jesus after Barnabas stood up for his authentic trust in Jesus.

CHARACTER THAT MAKES A DIFFERENCE SEES BEYOND THE FEARS OF OTHERS TO SEE PEOPLE FOR WHO THEY ARE IN CHRIST. Barnabas came alongside Saul of Tarsus and vouched for his authentic conversion when others doubted the sincerity of his faith. Fear clouded the judgment of the early believers. Those whom Saul had come to put in jail were rightfully skeptical of welcoming him to their fellowship. Barnabas's relationship to God helped him see past the fear of others and come alongside Paul who would ultimately take the message of Jesus to all people groups.

Jessica (not her real name) is a modern-day Barnabas. Several years ago, as she was dropping by the local coffee shop to collect day-old pastries (to take to a women's shelter), one of the workers came to her and asked to talk to her. The worker had seen Jessica day after day serve in this way and had come to trust her smile and friendly conversation. As the worker shared her story, Jessica discovered the girl had grown up in a family mired in generational Satanism, and she was looking to get out of this horrible circumstance. It was a huge risk to expose her situation to Jessica, but the worker sensed that she could trust Jessica. Her sense was true.

Imagine how I (Gene) felt when I heard the story. Could this be true? Could a person living in such abuse work two blocks from our church? How would the church respond when her story got out? But I trusted Jessica, her love for people, and her gift of discernment. When I met the worker, she was everything Jessica had described her to be, and we went to work praying for and supporting her deliverance from this wickedness. Recently the worker celebrated her seventh year of freedom from her family and those who had abused her. The journey has been dangerous and with some painful setbacks, but she continues to grow in her relationship with Jesus because a *daughter of encouragement* listened to her story and invited the church to come alongside her.

The next time we see Barnabas in the Book of Acts is when he encouraged the church in Antioch. The leaders in Jerusalem heard about the outbreak of God's love among the people of Antioch, and they sent Barnabas, whom they trusted, to see what was going on. When he arrived, he saw the hand of God creating a new people. Having observed "the grace of God" in the church as people from all walks of life and religious backgrounds trusted Jesus as the Messiah, he knew the church needed solid teaching about the things of God. Luke, the writer of Acts, tells us that the *son of encouragement* intentionally traveled to Tarsus, Saul's hometown, found him, and encouraged him to come and teach the new followers of Jesus in Antioch (Acts 11:25). Saul agreed, and after a time of teaching with Barnabas in Antioch, Luke records that it was there that the Christ-followers were first called *Christians*. ONE MAN'S ENCOURAGEMENT FOR ANOTHER MAN TO INVEST HIS GIFT IN THE WORK OF GOD CHANGED THE WORLD!

Barnabas also came alongside the church in Jerusalem during a time of famine (Acts 11:27–30). The Antioch church chose Barnabas and his companion Saul to take a gift, collected from the church, to aid those in distress by the food shortage. During that time, he connected with John Mark and invited him to join what God was doing to expand the Good News of Jesus to all peoples. Later, after his first missionary journey with Saul, now called Paul, Barnabas with his partner in ministry described what God had done to invite non-Jewish men and women into the family of God (Acts 15:12). In the face of heated opposition, Barnabas came alongside his partner in ministry and defended the work of the Holy Spirit among the new people groups.

We have already seen how Barnabas befriended John Mark (see the chapter on John Mark in the "How God Develops Character" section) after their separation from Paul. This act of support for the weaker person is characteristic of Christ's love in the heart of those who trust Him. The *son of encouragement* came alongside this young leader to restore him to worth and ministry.

CHARACTER THAT MAKES A DIFFERENCE ENCOURAGES BELIEVERS TO USE THEIR SKILLS TO MEET THE NEEDS OF OTHERS. When Barnabas saw the spiritual needs of the new converts to Christianity in Antioch, he traveled to Tarsus to recruit Saul to teach them the Scriptures. Barnabas could have taken on the task himself, but his character allowed others more skilled than him to fill the need. The *son of encouragement* invited Saul to join what God was doing among the church in Antioch and thus allowed God to put in place a man who would carry the Good News of Jesus to the ends of the earth. Christlike character encourages others to become part of what God is doing to change the hearts of people.

How did Barnabas get his heart of encouragement that comes alongside others? The Bible described Barnabas as "a good man, full of the Holy Spirit and faith" (Acts 11:24). When Jesus told His disciples He was going away, He promised to send "another advocate" (John 14:16). This advocate, or Helper (NASB), was the Holy Spirit. The name Jesus chose to describe the Holy Spirit whom He would send literally meant to "one called alongside." Jesus promised that upon His return to the Father, He would send another like Him to come alongside His disciples—the Holy Spirit. His purpose was, and still is, to empower them to carry out His call on their lives. This same Holy Spirit filled the heart of Barnabas, and he reflected the Holy Spirit's work in his life as he came alongside others.

We know from Scripture that one of the manifestations, or gifts, of the Holy Spirit in a disciple's life is "encouragement" (Romans 12:8). The root word for this gift is the same one Jesus chose to describe the Holy Spirit. It follows, then, that the *son of encouragement* exhibited the gift of the Holy Spirit whose very nature is that of coming alongside those who trust in Him. God equipped Barnabas to empower and encourage those he met to be who God created them to be in Christ Jesus. Barnabas got his heart of encouragement because the Holy Spirit lived and manifested Himself in his heart. That same Holy Spirit dwells in the lives of those who trust Jesus today.

Part of a Christian's character is the active presence of the Holy Spirit in his or her life. We often neglect the powerful role the manifestation of the Holy Spirit plays in the life of a follower of Jesus. The Holy Spirit equips us to serve the church and its global mission. When we consider the character of a Christian, we must include the role of the Holy Spirit as He motivates and empowers the Christian to teach, serve, encourage, lead, and proclaim the Good News of Jesus.

God used Barnabas to take the message of Jesus to the ends of the earth. His character made a lasting difference in the lives of millions because he demonstrated the heart of God.

A Challenge for Our Day

- Does your character portray a generous heart? Would others consider you a person of integrity who reflects the heart of God? How have you demonstrated the giving heart of God?
- Who have you come alongside of to take up their case in the face of fear or distrust from others?
- Who have you invited to join God where He is working? How have you encouraged others to complete tasks that you could do but would be best done by those more skilled and empowered by God to complete?

Further Study

Spend some time reading about Barnabas in a Bible dictionary or encyclopedia. Record some of what you find in your journal.

- You may want to dig deeper into the biblical concept of spiritual gifts. Read the following passages of Scripture to get a grasp on the gifts God gives His people to complete His call on their lives: Romans 12:3–8; 1 Corinthians 12–14; Ephesians 4:11–13; 1 Peter 4:10.
- Add to this case study what you learned about Barnabas in the case study of John Mark. What more did you learn about Barnabas's character from that story?

CHAPTER 16

Stephen:
Character That Is
Fearless

B oth of us have served as pastors in a local church. At least once during our ministry we have faced a group of people who angrily resisted what we believed God would have us do as a church. Those who opposed our leadership decision(s) offered their alternatives to members both privately and publicly, and they sometimes attacked our integrity or character as part of the argument. When faced with this opposition that came to us in our office, a hallway, or in a public meeting of the church, fear erupted in our hearts. And we had good reasons to be afraid. These particular people could not only get us fired, they could make life difficult for our families, not to mention ruin the reputation of the church in the community because of a nasty church fight. Fear became a true enemy of faithfulness and courage in the face of concerted efforts to curtail God's direction for the church. Trust in God's purposes for the church and us—built upon a personal, ongoing relationship with God—became the primary source of confidence when all else had been stripped from us. Character built upon trust became our fortress of courage in the face of hostile opposition.

What experience have you faced where fear could have paralyzed your actions, but where your trust in God helped you to be true to your convictions?

When we read the story of the early church, we see that almost every Spirit-filled disciple of Jesus faced opposition. Peter, James, and John were imprisoned, beaten, and even killed by those opposed to their witness to Jesus as the Christ and risen Lord. Jesus taught His disciples that they would be blessed in God's eyes when others persecuted them on His behalf. In His inaugural address to His disciples, He said,

Blessed are you when people insult you, persecute you and falsely say all kinds of evil against you because of me. Rejoice and be glad, because great is your reward in heaven, for in the same way they persecuted the prophets who were before you.
—MATTHEW 5:11–12

Persecution and resistance to God's leadership among His people was to be expected by those who served on the front line of the Holy Spirit's movement called the early church.

We who have lived in the West have adopted a view of our lives that favors comfort and having things our way. David Platt in his insightful book *Radical* challenges American Christians by stating that we "are starting to redefine Christianity. We are giving in to the dangerous temptation to take the Jesus of the Bible and twist him into a version of Jesus we are more comfortable with." We want Jesus to be and act like we expect Him to be and act. But when we read the New Testament, we discover Jesus is not who we always expect Him to be nor does He act the way acceptable people would act in our culture.

We fear the threat of those who would challenge our faith or even attack our positions of belief and lifestyle. We want our lives to work the way we have designed them. Isn't that what career and project planning are about? Yet, when we see the true Jesus as revealed in Scripture, we see we cannot invariably anticipate His actions or words. Sometimes He is in the chaos and threats in life rather than in our trips to Disney World. Mark Galli, senior editor of *Christianity Today*, observed that the chaos of life may be

God's way of molding us into forgiving and loving people:

Jesus refuses to be put in a religious box. He's not a nice Savior, whose goal is to make us feel better about ourselves and become well-adjusted, productive members of society. All that is well and good, and it is part of our lot in life. But this is not the mission of Jesus. He's not interested in nice, well-adjusted people, but mostly in people who forgive and love. And sometimes he has to bring a little chaos into our lives to help us become the people he's called us to be. Chaos and discomfort can be God's tools to change us into the likeness of Jesus.

In the Acts of the Apostles, Stephen, one of the seven chosen to serve the needs of the church (Acts 6:1–6), was stoned to death by the religious authorities because of his witness to Jesus. He experienced the chaos of religious hatred and the violence of a lynch mob, and he became the first martyr of the church. However, in the turmoil at the end of his life, his character shone through as evidence of the Holy Spirit in his life. The miracles performed through him, his Spirit-guided wise answers to his accusers, and his calm faith in the face of a riotous mob that hurled insults and stones at him demonstrated a Christlike character that spoke loudly of Jesus' love and forgiveness. Enduring faith, not paralyzing fear, gave him the strength to be a bold witness to Jesus to the end. Let's look at his character and how it impacted others.

Evidence of Character

Biblical character that makes a difference is the result of the presence of the Holy Spirit in our lives. Such character shows itself as calm in the middle of a storm and peaceful in an angry riot. We have seen how dependence upon God (Moses) and sitting at the feet of Jesus (Mary and Martha) create in us character that God uses to reveal His purposes to others. The biblical record does not reveal to us how Stephen got his fearless character, but we can observe the evidence of his shining character.

A Servant's Heart

People choose those who demonstrate godly character and service to be their leaders and to serve their needs. For example, when the apostles asked the people to pick from among themselves seven men to meet the need of feeding the Greek-speaking widows in Jerusalem, the people chose Stephen as one of the seven. Most likely from the neighborhood of those in need, he was the only one that Luke described as "a man full of faith and of the Holy Spirit" (Acts 6:5). His peers recognized the presence of God in Stephen's life and that he was a man of faith.

How do your peers see you? Be honest. Do they choose you when they need someone with a servant's heart?

Later, when Stephen began to minister among the people we are told he performed "great wonders and signs." Again, Luke noted he was "a man full of God's grace and power" (Acts 6:8). Stephen's fullness in God's grace and power was the basis of the signs he demonstrated among the people. His personal relationship with God formed the foundation of his public acts of service and miracles in the lives of others. We fool ourselves if we think we can perform similar acts without an ongoing, personal relationship with God.

Stephen's servant heart and Spirit-filled life formed the foundation of his character, which others turned to in times of need. God used him to demonstrate His power and presence in people's lives as he performed wonders and signs among the people.

Spirit-Guided Wisdom

Another evidence of Stephen's character was his ability to answer wisely the false accusations from others. Opposition from fellow Jewish men in a local synagogue arose against Stephen. His witness and demonstration of God's power among the people led those who did not accept his actions to attack him. They argued with him about whether Jesus was the Messiah, Jesus' teachings about the Law and Temple, and Jesus' death and resurrection. Stephen trusted in Jesus as the Christ, he had been baptized, and was full of the Holy Spirit. His opponents did not understand the true meaning of Jesus' life and death. But, Luke noted, they could not stand up against the "wisdom the Spirit gave him as he spoke" (Acts 6:10). *Godly character exhibits godly wisdom.* In the whirlwind of attack and argument, God provided the wisdom Stephen needed to be a bold witness for Christ.

This wisdom was not from Stephen. It came from the Holy Spirit and was promised to all who trust Jesus. Christ promised His followers that people would seize them, and they would find themselves before "kings and governors . . . all on account of my name" (Luke 21:12). There they would bear witness to Him. Jesus, however, encouraged them by saying:

But make up your mind not to worry beforehand how you will defend yourselves. For I will give you words and wisdom that none of your adversaries will be able to resist or contradict. You will be betrayed even by parents, brothers and sisters, relatives and friends, and they will put some of you to death. Everyone

will hate you because of me. But not a hair of your head will perish. Stand firm, and you will win life.
—LUKE 21:14–19

Stephen followed Jesus' teachings and example when he trusted the Spirit to give him the words to speak as he faced his accusers. His opponents could not stand up against such godly wisdom and impeccable character.

An Angelic Countenance

When the opposition could not overcome Stephen with their arguments, they enlisted others to attack his integrity. They accused him of speaking falsely "against Moses and against God" (Acts 6:11). Their lies stirred up the people, and they took him before the Sanhedrin, a sort of Supreme Court among the Jewish people. Once he was in front of the religious leaders, more false witnesses accused Stephen of blasphemy against the Temple and the Law (vv. 13–14). You'll remember that they said the same thing when accusing Jesus according to Acts, Stephen remained silent during the initial tirades against him. Yet, he still bore witness of God's presence in his life. How did he do that?

The Bible says that as the religious leaders looked intently upon Stephen they saw that his face was "like the face of an angel" (Acts 6:15). What was it about Stephen that made his face look like that of an angel? Since we don't have detailed descriptions of angels' faces in the Bible, we can assume there was a shining or glowing of his face that caught their attention. We know of "a man in shining clothes" appearing to the Roman centurion Cornelius later in Acts (Acts 10:30). This man was most likely an angel messenger of God. Like Moses whose face shone after being with God on the mountain

(Exodus 34:29–30), and Jesus' shining face during his transfiguration (Luke 9:29), Stephen's face glowed with the presence of the Holy Spirit. The Spirit's character that dwelt in him had grown in his character, and those who looked upon him saw a difference in his face.

Those who exhibit godly character do not necessarily have literal shining faces. They do, however, glow with the countenance of the One who fills their heart. This may come in the form of a genuine smile, or eyes that shine with hope in the midst of tough times. Their lives illuminate the darkness with their words and actions. The Bible teaches that "God is light; in him there is no darkness at all" (1 John 1:5). If God is light, then we can expect that God's Spirit would shine through those who trusted Him and were filled "with God's grace and power." Jesus taught His disciples they (and we) are "the light of the world," and He told them (and us) to "let your light shine before others, that they may see your good deeds and glorify your Father in heaven" (Matthew 5:16). The light of our "good deeds" and bold witness shines before our neighbors, community, and church, and illuminates the way to glorify God.

A Bold Witness

Stephen took the opportunity when he stood before the religious leaders to witness boldly to who Jesus was. His message to the leaders is the longest recorded speech in Acts, and it rehearses God's encounter with His people from Abraham up to the time Solomon built the Temple (Acts 7:1–47). They listened quietly until he—like Jesus—taught that the Temple was no longer the dwelling place of God and that they had "betrayed and murdered" the Righteous One, or the Messiah (7:48–52). Rather than seeking to protect his own life or promising to stop what he was accused of doing, Stephen took the opportunity before the religious leaders to explain history from God's perspective. He courageously called them to consider their actions toward Jesus and judge whether or not they had missed the work of God among them.

Stephen was not filled with fear that day before his opponents. He was filled with the Holy Spirit, and he boldly shared the truth of God. Although the atmosphere and stacked witnesses could have made him fearful, this servant of God stepped up and told the truth about what God had done. He called the leaders to conviction about their actions and insisted they trust Jesus to be who He said He was. While he pushed for their repentance and trust in Jesus, he got something much the opposite—their anger in return.

Christlike Peace and Forgiveness in the Face of Death

When the religious leaders heard Stephen's accusations of their disobedience, they stormed Stephen and dragged him outside to be stoned. You might expect a lone victim to put up a fight or resist their unjust behavior, but God blessed Stephen with a vision of the One who had empowered him to speak fearlessly. Luke tells us that in middle of the riot to have him killed, Stephen looked to heaven and saw "Jesus standing at the right hand of God" (Acts 7:55). The glorified, ascended Christ waited to receive His faithful servant. Stephen told those who seized him what he had seen, but they were only more incensed and dragged him outside the city and began to stone him (vv. 56–58).

As his accusers bombarded him with stones of all sizes, he did not defend himself or plead for mercy. Like his Leader who died for him, this servant of God humbly asked God to receive his spirit and to forgive those who threw the stones at him (v. 60). The Bible says, "When he had said this, he fell asleep." Not once did Stephen show fear of those who attacked him or even of death itself. Was this possible because he was a strong personality or because he had some superhuman resolve in him that gave him this lack of fear in the face of death?

The Bible makes it clear that the source of Stephen's fearlessness was the Holy Spirit. Three times in the stories about him, the Bible records that he was "full of God's grace and power" or "full of the Holy Spirit" (Acts 6:5, 8; 7:55). He was not an exceptional man with personal charisma or confidence in his beliefs. He was filled with the Holy Spirit who allowed him to speak truth wisely, witness boldly, and to face death peacefully. Stephen's character displayed the character of God through the Spirit of God, and that Spirit who gave him a servant's heart and courage.

Stephen's story is not just an ancient story of early church martyrs. His story is told over and over even today. Followers of Jesus continue to face opposition and death for their trust in Jesus as the Son of God. We have seen firsthand the persecution of Christians in communist and atheist or religiously intolerant countries. Imprisonment and even death are still possibilities for those who boldly witness to Jesus today. There were more martyrs in the twentieth century than all previous 19 centuries, and those numbers will continue to grow as the evil one continues to resist the movement of the Spirit in the lives of people. However, God's people need not cower in fear of these threats. The Spirit who empowered Stephen is the same Spirit who fills Christ followers today. No matter the chaos or opponents to the Gospel you face today, you can have the same power, boldness, and humility as Stephen.

A Challenge for Our Day

- What do you face today that brings fear into your heart? Offer that in prayer to God and ask that the Holy Spirit empower you to face that situation with courage and humility.
- Take time to pray for your Christian brothers and sisters around the world who face persecution, imprisonment, and even death for their trust in Jesus, the Christ. Ask God to give them the wisdom and peace He gave Stephen.
- In what ways have you been a shining face to others? Do you "let your light so shine before others that they may see your good works and glorify your Father who is in heaven"? How can you do that today?

Further Study

Read Acts 6 and 7 in order to see the full story of Stephen and how God used him to advance the Christian church in its early years.

- Look up terms such as Sanhedrin, the practice of stoning, and some of the biblical characters mentioned in Stephen's speech to gain a deeper understanding of their role in God's history with His people.
- Read about the other six men chosen by the church to serve the widows in Jerusalem (Acts 6:1–6). Which names besides Stephen's are mentioned again after they are listed? How did God use them to widen the influence of the church "to the ends of the earth"?

CHAPTER 17

Paul and Timothy: Character That Leaves a Legacy

T
he goal of the Christian life is *not* to "get it right" so you can "get into heaven." Our trust in the free grace of God shown in the person of His Son, Jesus, is what makes us right before Holy God and ensures that we live abundant and eternal lives in Christ Jesus. We live to love God and serve others. As a friend of Gene's put it, "We are saved to serve." Our lives are not our own. We have been bought with a price (1 Corinthians 6:20); therefore, we are to share and serve as servants of Jesus, the Christ. In the context of our writing about character, we believe we are not simply to allow God and others to mold our character, but there will come a time when God will use us to mold the character of another person. This chapter gives us some hints how to do that as we observe the life and ministry of the Apostle Paul.

When Paul wrote to his brothers and sisters in Christ in the city of Thessalonica, he reminded them, "You are witnesses, and so is God, of how devoutly, righteously, and blamelessly we behaved toward you believers" (1 Thessalonians 2:10 NASB). Paul described his behavior while among his friends as a platform for their trust in him. What he mentions in that verse are matters of character, the heart of what we have been writing about in this book.

Few leadership and discipleship manuals discuss the character of the leader. We believe, however, that the leader's character is key in helping people move through the apparent chaos of leaving the past behind and pressing forward to the future. The character of the leader can help or hinder the leader's message. Faulty character can damage progress made toward

God's vision for a person's life. The character of the leader is where God's work in that person's life is most evident. Whether you are in a leadership position or not, your character displays itself on the stage of life.

When people observe you, they should see in you—like Paul—a humble heart, pure motives, and actions that are not self-serving. Followers will engage the mission and pursue the vision when these character traits are present in you as their leader. The secular world realizes this truth. Businesses, schools, and communities have begun to emphasize character development as part of what they produce. Faith-based groups like Character First offer training and resources in this area of personal development. It is time God's people begin to place an emphasis on character development at the church, at home, and in the world.

Paul staked his ministry to the Thessalonians on his character. His enemies argued with his methodology and even his theology, but they could not assail his character. He guarded it jealously and referred to it as a defense against those who slandered him. Throughout his letters he insisted that how he acted with those he wrote told of his love, encouragement, patience and care for them.

READ 1 THESSALONIANS 2:5–10. How did Paul describe his ministry among them? What did this say about his character?

Actions That Reveal Character

Paul reminded his readers that when he came to them his motives were pure. He "never used flattery," nor did he "put on a mask to cover up greed" (1 Thessalonians 2:5). God was his witness to how he conducted himself among them. He not only shared his message, "the gospel of God," but he shared his life with them as well (v. 8). Paul refused to make his message the only focus of his ministry. He cared for his brothers and sisters in Christ enough to share his life with them. *Message plus a shared life equal authentic ministry.* Finally, he was able to point to his behavior as indication of his pure motive and desire to serve them. He challenged them to remember "how devoutly, righteously, and blamelessly" he conducted himself among them (1 Thessalonians 2:10 NASB).

Genuine servant leaders and disciples live lives that can be described as "devout, righteous and blameless." These are not signs of moral perfection, but of their pursuit of holiness in their lives. A servant leader or disciple is devout when he or she honors the things of God above all other values. A servant leader or disciple is righteous when he or she chooses the right over the easy and benchmarks his or her choice against the righteousness of God revealed in Scripture. Such individuals are blameless when their actions are unassailable by critics and accountability partners alike. Godly character demonstrates itself in daily life as devotion to God, righteous living, and blameless motives toward others. Paul is our biblical example of such a life.

Molding the Character of Others

The apostle did not use his character as an argument for people to trust him alone. Paul instilled these character values in his apprentice, Timothy. We meet Timothy at the beginning of Paul's second journey into the global mission field of non-Jewish peoples (Acts 16:1). Timothy's mother (as well as his grandmother) was a follower of Jesus and an ethnic Jew (2 Timothy 1:5). His father was neither. Paul circumcised Timothy in order to make his ministry among both the Jews and Greeks more effective (v. 3). Luke also tells us that Christians "at Lystra and Iconium spoke well of him" (Acts 16:2). Timothy had a good reputation that had been built upon his relationship with the Lord, as taught and modeled by his mother and grandmother. Paul saw this in him and he invited him to join him in what God was doing in the movement of the Holy Spirit.

Timothy became a trusted companion of Paul. He traveled with Paul into what is now Europe, and Paul left him with Silas in Berea to build up the church while Paul went on to Athens (Acts 17:14). He later joined Paul in Corinth (Acts 18:5), and he accompanied the senior missionary on his third missionary journey. When Paul made his final trip to Jerusalem to share the collection for the poor he had taken among the ethnic Christians during his travels, Timothy was among his trusted ambassadors (Acts 20:4). Paul chose Timothy to lead the church in Ephesus, and while he was in prison in Rome, Paul corresponded with this young pastor in order to train him for ministry and to mold his character.

Paul, for example, taught his protégé not to let anyone look down on him for his youth but to be an example for those in his care "in speech, in conduct, in faith, in love and in purity" (1 Timothy 4:12). Character is exposed in our speech, how we act, in whom we put our trust, and whether or not our lives are pure in the things of the Lord. We do not want to be seen as "whitewashed tombs, which appear beautiful on the outside, but on the inside are full of the bones of the dead and everything unclean" (Matthew 23:27). Paul challenged Timothy to demonstrate godly character through what he said, how he acted, how he trusted God daily, and by living a pure life before others. Timothy's character, lived out before others, would not allow them to "look down on him."

Pure and Blameless

Paul wrote in another letter that God's people should be "pure and blameless for the day of Christ" (Philippians 1:10). Writing to the church in Philippi, Paul insisted that his motive to serve grew solely out of an "obligation to preach." He was not self-serving in any way. He acknowledged that some preach out of "envy and rivalry, but others out of good will" (Philippians 1:15). Some speak "out of rivalry." Others preach "out of false motives or true" (Philippians 1:18). He brought the message of Christ to them because of his call, not out of his need to compete with others or from motives that were not true to his mission.

A primary tenet of Paul's defense of his character was that he vowed he did "not peddle the word of God" (2 Corinthians 2:17). He had an intense commitment to present the gospel without compensation, which was his "right" as an itinerant teacher. He intentionally gave that up to be free to say what needed to be said. He argued with those who assailed his character in Corinth that he did not use his "right" to be supported by them. He said he had "not used any of these rights," but his "boast" was to "preach the gospel and offer it free of charge" (1 Corinthians 9:12–18). Paul demonstrated a character born out of the free grace of Christ, and he refused to live in obligation to others or them to him.

Take a moment to think about Paul's character. Based on the passages we have discussed and what you know of Paul's character, make a list of his most notable character traits. What claims did he make that you can make about your character? How does your character line up to these traits?

The Crucible of Character

The most clear indicator of a person's character is shown by his or her words and actions. Character reveals itself as *consistent behavior under pressure.* Behavior is what people see, and it is the clearest indicator of your character. God used the "silent years" of Paul's ministry after he was converted to prepare him for his mission. As he began to share the good news of Jesus in Damascus and Arabia, God used the quiet times and crucible of conflict to prepare him for the public ministry that would follow. This period of some isolation was part of God's development of his character.

Hard times shape character. Hard times also *expose* character. Conflict and opposition in your life can create a crucible of character development. Character is created by the "yes" and "no" you choose every day in the context of conflict. Paul taught from his personal experience that "affliction produces endurance," and it is endurance that produces "proven character" (Romans 5:3–4 HCSB). Character proven over time and tested in tough times is what produces hope in those who trust Jesus (Romans 5:5). That kind of hope never fails. Like a runner training for a marathon, the "affliction" of training produces the endurance necessary to carry the athlete through to the end of the race. That endurance, when maintained, results in proven results race after race.

Paul paradoxically boasted of his weakness that came from trials. His confession became that when he was weak, Christ was strong. He would boast in his weaknesses rather than his strengths because it was when he was helpless that Christ's character shone brightest through his life and ministry (2 Corinthians 12:10). He came to know that the "treasure" of salvation was held in fragile "clay jars" (2 Corinthians 4:7). Hard times created a humble heart in the apostle. He claimed Christ's success through his life was a result of the difficulties he faced. Paul did not avoid or whine over the conflicts in his life and ministry. He saw them as the places in which God demonstrated His greatest power. We who long for an easy life may long for the wrong thing. Resistance to the struggles of life may be God's way of giving us ultimately what we truly long for: character that reflects Christ.

Paul asked for prayer to be bold in whatever situation he found himself, not to be released from it (Ephesians 6:19-20). He did not ask his friends to pray that God would get him out of prison when he wrote to the Ephesian Christians. He asked that they pray that while he was in prison he would be a bold witness. This attitude reflects character dependent upon Christ, and it is a different perspective from that of those who believe God's will always includes the removal of pain. In another example, Paul told the Corinthians to stay in the situation they were in when Christ found them (1 Corinthians 7). Even new Christians in old marriages (if married to a pagan) were to stay in that marriage in order to demonstrate Christ's love to an unbelieving spouse and family. Changing settings is not what makes you bold—boldness comes from accepting your situation and demonstrating Christlike character wherever you are. This is why Paul was happy to be "an ambassador in chains" (Ephesians 6:20), an odd title for leaders in American Christianity today.

How has God used hard times in your life to develop your character? What are some confessions you stand upon that have come from those times of testing?

Spiritual Authority and an Open Heart

Character molded in the rough and tumble of daily faith is the basis for *spiritual authority.* It is a by-product of a mature character developed through a maturing process. Servant leaders and followers of Jesus who serve God's call on their lives and lead by serving those on mission with them exhibit mature character and discover they have an authority they did not set out to gain. Authority to lead wherever God has placed you flows from a daily pursuit of God. Experiencing God in the daily thoughts, choices, and activities of the day is the path to authority for those who lead and serve. Spiritual authority flows out of character that has been influenced by the Spirit of God in a personal, daily relationship with Him.

Another byproduct of character born out of adversity is an *open heart.* On one hand, trials can cause a disciple to encase his or her heart in an iron box where no one can see the wounds and pain. This iron-boxed condition of the heart keeps an apprentice of Jesus from empathizing with the loss of others. They can develop a "just get over it" attitude toward those who are struggling through changes related to life. When the heart of the communicator has been hardened, the message is hard to hear! People's feelings don't matter much to the one who has lost them himself.

Adversity, on the other hand, can also result in an open heart. Character based on such openness is transparent, vulnerable, and willing to step into the world of those who are hurting. Many servants and leaders in ministry are tempted to survive a situation in a numbed state. Addictions, sadly, are as common among Christians as the rest of the population. Rather than connecting to people, the wounded withdraw to doctor their wounds. Left alone, they do not find the healing that God offers us in the Holy Spirit-led community called the church. An open heart allows the adversities they experience to train them in godliness and to mold their character into the likeness of Christ in order that they may help mold that same character in the lives of others.

What is the path to character that allows the message to be heard and the mission to be central? It is service to God's call on your life. A servant's heart is at the core of the character of a disciple who makes a difference in the kingdom of God. Service is the path to become like Jesus, our Mentor. Service is the test of character as well as the path to Christlike character. To refuse to serve God's call on your life for the sake of others is to expose a pride-filled heart. It is no longer about God's call on your life. Everything becomes about you, and that is the beginning of the end of your ministry and effectiveness as a follower of Jesus.

A Challenge for Our Day

- Paul claimed he walked among those he served "devoutly, righteously, and blamelessly." Which of these character traits matches your walk? Who is watching your life and may be influenced by it?
- Paul molded the character of his young mentee, Timothy. Into whom are you investing your life so that he or she may serve and lead others in your absence?
- Hard times expose our true character. How have the tough experiences molded your character? Or have they wounded you so deeply you are unable to serve others? Present your situation to God and ask, as Paul did, that you be bold in your circumstances so others may see the power of Christ in your life.

Further Study

Take some time to dig a little deeper into the life of Paul and Timothy to see how God developed character that left a legacy.

- Read Acts 16–20 to see how God used these two servants to widen the message of Jesus to the known world.
- Read 1 Timothy, Paul's letter from prison to his protégé, and note the ways in which the senior missionary developed the character of this young pastor.
- Return to the passages from Paul's letters in this chapter and read the contexts around them in order to see the full message of God's Word in those locations.

CHAPTER 18

Philemon:
Character That
Refreshes Hearts

One thing that we can count on as we work with groups or serve in organizations is that we will face times of crisis. Regardless of how much preparation and planning we do, we face issues and conflicts that have great potential to cause strife and division. Over the years with both of us serving as pastors, we can testify that around every corner is an opportunity for conflict in the church. This is also true in the home, workplace, or really anyplace where people have to interact and work together. In these times of crisis, how important is it to have access to someone you can trust to make clear decisions which honor God and defuse difficult situations? A person's character will often determine if the crisis is escalated or defused.

However, this kind of character is not something that develops overnight in an individual. Rather, it comes from a continual growing relationship with Christ. One aspect of the kind of character that can be counted on to honor God in a crisis is that it is a character that is steadfast and reliable to everyone. Think about the people around you. When a difficult situation or a potential problem needs to be addressed, who do you call upon? It is individuals who have shown over the years that they love the Lord and, from this love, they have a proven track record of honoring God and encouraging others to do the same.

The Book of Philemon provides an example of one man with a reputation of loving God and loving those around him. In Philemon, the smallest book of the New Testament, the Apostle Paul provides a brief description of Philemon's character that serves as a challenge for anyone who desires be used by God in the midst of turmoil.

Background to the Story

The Book of Philemon has been considered more of a "postcard" than a letter in the New Testament. The reason for this short note was due to a runaway slave named Onesimus who had stolen from Philemon and evidently fled to Rome. Apparently Onesimus came in contact with the Apostle Paul and became a Christian. While Paul wanted to keep Onesimus with him in Rome, he understood that the runaway slave needed to return to Philemon and the church at Colosse. Can you imagine some of the potential problems that could occur in the life of this church at the return of Onesimus? First, he had stolen from Philemon and was a runaway slave in the Roman Empire. These offences could be punishable by death. At the least, the law required that this criminal be dealt with harshly. However, this criminal was now a brother in Christ. In fact, there must have been a drastic change in the life of this man to go all the way back to Colosse knowing that he could be legally executed for his past deeds. Can you see the potential crisis? Would the congregation divide on this issue? We do not know the feelings of the church, but we think it is safe to assume that some may have felt that the Roman law needed to be upheld while others believed things should be overlooked now that Onesimus was a fellow believer in Christ.

Paul sent Onesimus back to Philemon with a simple letter stating that the slave had become a Christian and asked that he be taken back into the household as a Christian brother. Paul does not demand what must be done, but simply appeals to what he knows of Philemon's character and then offers to personally repay any debt or loss that Philemon has incurred from the theft. With such an important issue, one that could have easily impacted the church at Colosse, Paul leaves the decision in the hands of Philemon based on what he knows about the man's character.

READ PHILEMON 1–25.

A Closer Look at the Text

The Book of Philemon has often been overlooked because of the very focused and limited topic of the letter. The letter is dealing with a subject to which most people in our day cannot relate: slavery. However, for our study we simply want to look at what it was about Philemon that gave Paul a confident trust he would do the right thing in the middle of this controversy. We can find this answer in verses 4–7.

Paul makes his appeal based on what he has continued to hear about Philemon. Before we look at verse four, think about what others continue to hear about you. What do you think is said about the way you walk with the Lord as well as with other Christians? When there is a closed meeting to discuss a potential problem or issue at your church or workplace, do you think people "breathe a sigh of relief" knowing that you are there and will bring about a stability and peace because of your character and your proven track record in walking with God and others? Paul is thanking God for Philemon continually (vv. 4–5) because of what he hears about this man.

We get our first glimpse into what Paul is hearing about Philemon in verse 5. There is some discussion on how to understand verse 5, and we will not take time to discuss all of the varied opinions; rather, we take one of the most recognized understandings. Paul writes that he was hearing "about your love for all his holy people and your faith in the Lord Jesus." This was not a single event of hearing about his faith, but of Paul continuing to hear reports on the way in which Philemon believed and trusted in God. In this statement we see one of the processes in which God develops our character in a way that impacts His kingdom. This ongoing faith in the

Lord was being expressed in a love for the saints. The longer that we walk in faith, trusting in God, the greater the opportunity He has to shape our heart. The more we trust Him, and through confident faith, let Him form our character, the more we will see God's love flowing through our lives to others. There is a challenge here to look for evidence in our own lives of the love of God flowing through us to love those around us. Paul did not trust Philemon simply because he was a decent person or had a compassionate personality. Paul trusted this critical situation to Philemon because there was clear evidence this man loved the people in authentic Christian love.

Paul prayed that Philemon would respond to Onesimus based on this same faith in God and love for the saints, that it would be active and effective and there would be a greater understanding of all the goodness in Christ through Philemon's response. Certainly Paul was hopeful, for not only the restoration of the runaway slave, but through this entire ordeal the whole church would come to experience a greater understanding of the goodness of being a child of God. Should there be a different response to Onesimus from a Christian brother? Probably in most households in the city, he would have been severely punished at least, if not put to death. Is there a difference in how you respond when you have been wronged? Should a Christian act differently toward someone who has genuinely repented and wants to correct their mistakes?

Paul was not only thankful for what he knew and heard about Philemon's character, but this man's actions among his fellow Christians served as a source of joy to the apostle (v. 7). This joy was produced by the knowledge that Philemon's love had "refreshed the hearts of the Lord's people." We see that he has a deep faith in God that produced a love for the saints and this love was a source of refreshment to the people in his church. This is certainly a characteristic that is needed in our day. How many people need their hearts refreshed? How many people are worn out with the issues of life, feeling like there is no hope or are overwhelmed? At a time where Christians were being persecuted, having their property taken, and were looked at with general disapproval, Philemon was taking an active role to encourage his fellow believers in Christ. From this brief description of Philemon's character, it is evident why Paul could safely encourage Onesimus to return to face Philemon.

Character Revealed in Love for the Saints

Paul's description of Philemon reveals why the apostle had such confidence in his friend. Paul states that he could have simply commanded that Philemon accept Onesimus back and not punish him for his wrong doings. The apostle certainly had the authority in the church to make such a demand on behalf of the new Christian. However, as Paul realized, there was no need to make these demands of Philemon. Rather, Paul appealed based on love (v. 9), something he knew Philemon would understand. Paul had ongoing reports of the way Philemon loved the believers who met at his house church (v. 2)

We see this character revealed in several aspects. First, Philemon had a well-deserved reputation as a person of faith in God. This was not simply a faith that led to salvation, but a faith that caused him to be radically involved in the lives of others. We see this in the fact that the Colossian church gathered at his home. We can talk about our faith or claim to have faith, but genuine deep-seated faith in God leads to outward expression toward God's people as well as those outside of the church. The picture of Philemon's love refreshing the hearts of the saints is a wonderful example and challenge for every church member. He loved the people in a way that their lives were renewed or energized. We can assume that this was more than simply words of encouragement. He demonstrated a love toward them that strengthened and restored their lives. We don't think that just any casual encouragement would have brought "great joy" to the heart of Paul. This must have been something very special in the life of the church and the hearts of the people.

The Impact of Character

A CONSISTENT FAITH WALK WITH GOD CREATES OPPORTUNITIES TO BE USED TO BRING PEACE AND STABILITY TO DIFFICULT CIRCUMSTANCES. This situation had great potential for controversy in the church at Colosse. Should the runaway slave be punished? Roman law stated that a runaway could be put to death. How do you accept this man back into the household as well as the church? Certainly, Paul could have sent instructions with Onesimus on how they were to receive him back, but would this have settled all the controversy? How much more effective was it that the one who had been wronged receive Onesimus back and welcome him as a brother in Christ? Paul was able first to convince Onesimus to return home, and (second) to trust the outcome to Philemon based on the man's faith in God. From the text it does not seem like Paul had much to worry about as Philemon's continued faith was evident through his love and care for his fellow Christians. His faith in God expressed in his love for the saints would also be the basis to forgive and receive his new brother in Christ, as well as set an example for the entire local church.

GOD USES THE LOVING HEART AS A SOURCE OF REFRESHMENT TO THE WEARY OF HEART. We don't know of a more positive word about a fellow church member than to be known as a person who refreshes the hearts of the saints. Philemon's character had been shaped through faith, expressed through love, and it resulted in encouragement of others. In a time when so many were weary of the toils of life in the Roman world, he lived out his Christian faith in a way that revitalized those in his church. Philemon's walk with God and his deeds toward the people were also a source of joy and encouragement to the great apostle Paul.

GOD USES THE PERSON OF CHARACTER TO REDEEM PEOPLE. While we have been looking at Philemon's character, the heart of this little book is that this runaway slave had been transformed. Onesimus, the one who had previously been "useless" was now "useful" to the church at Colosse (v. 11). (The name Onesimus in Greek means "useful," so Paul was making a play on words.) He was now a fellow laborer in Christ. In the Book of Colossians, Paul calls him "our faithful and dear brother, who is one of you" (Colossians 4:9). For Onesimus to reach this potential, he would first encounter a great man of godly character, the apostle Paul, and then would need to be forgiven, encouraged, and accepted by another man of character: Philemon. Traditional understanding suggests that Onesimus became a leader in the Colossian church. However, this would not have been possible without a man of character's forgiveness and acceptance.

A Challenge for Our Day

The account of Philemon provides an example of an amazing church member. He had a deep faith in God that was expressed in a love for the people around him. His life serves as a challenge since his love brought joy to Paul and refreshed the hearts of the saints. In a day when so many people are struggling and weighed down with life, does your life refresh the hearts of others? What are people saying about you in the circles you travel? When a crisis or potentially difficult situation arises, are you one of the first people called to help? Are you trusted because of your proven love for people? Can God place you in the middle of difficult situations based on your past record of faith and love?

Further Study

- Look at 2 Kings 18–19 and examine how God used Isaiah to encourage King Hezekiah as he faced the Assyrian army.
- Take a moment to read Acts 15:1–35. Look at how God used Peter to defend Paul's and Barnabas' ministry to the Gentiles.

CHAPTER 19

Ruth:
Character That Is
Selflessly Loyal

T he Book of Ruth is a unique book in the Old Testament. In many ways it is an uneventful story as no major events of national consequence take place. However, what is extraordinary in the story is not so much the type of events that take place, but rather the character that is displayed by Ruth and Boaz. The Book of Ruth takes place during the period of the Judges (Ruth 1:1). This period is often referred to as the darkest period in Israelite history. If you remember much about the Book of Judges, there was a continual cycle the people of God encountered: 1) they sinned and departed from God, 2) God brought judgment on the people through foreign oppressors, 3) the people cried out to God, and finally 4) God would send a judge to deliver the people (see Judges 2:11–19). The problem was that once the judge (or champion) was gone, the people rebelled again and started the cycle all over again. Two phrases describe Israel during this period: "the Israelites did evil in the eyes of the Lord" and "in those days there was no king in Israel; everyone did as he saw fit. " During this time the people showed no loyalty toward God or toward each other. In fact, the only time the tribes of Israel were united in Judges was when 11 of 12 tribes joined together to destroy the tribe of Benjamin (Judges 20).

The Book of Ruth is set in stark contrast to the Book of Judges. While the nation as a whole was in dire straits in its relationship with God, there were still some who exhibited character and acted with integrity and loyalty to God and to others. This character shown in the text is expressed through the word *hesed* [pronounced KEH-sed] in the original language. This term means "covenant loyalty" and is often translated "loving-kindness." As you read through this short story, take notice of the instances and people that are described by this *loving-kindness:*

- Ruth's commitment to Naomi (1:16–17).
- This is the quality that Boaz notices in Ruth toward Naomi (2:12).
- Boaz is praised by Naomi for the *hesed* he shows (2:20).
- Boaz's negotiations with Ruth are centered on this idea (3:9–13).
- The Lord's *hesed* is introduced in 1:8–9 as a factor that will eventually lead to the successful remarriage of Naomi's daughter-in-law realized in Ruth 4:13.

In many ways the attitude toward God and the selfish nature of the people during Ruth's time parallel our day. In a day gripped by selfish ambition and a lack of care or faithfulness toward others in marriage, family, business, and community, the example of character exhibited in this little book serves as a refreshing challenge. When too often we are faced with the choice of looking out for our own interests or simply not getting involved, in the Book of Ruth we see examples of self-sacrifice and a dedication of loving-kindness that flows from the heart of God as well as through those dedicated to God.

The Story

The book is named for its principal character, Ruth the Moabite. Because of a famine, Elimelech of Bethlehem took his family to live in the near country Moab. He and his two sons died in the land of Moab leaving behind his widow, Naomi, and her two Moabite daughters-in-law, Ruth and Orpah. Naomi convinced Orpah to return to her family. However, Ruth insisted on returning to Bethlehem with Naomi.

The two widows returned in time for the harvest, and Ruth began to glean grain in the fields of Boaz. Boaz was a relative of Elimelech and through a series of clever dealings, Boaz was able to marry Ruth. They had a son together named Obed, therefore continuing the family line of Elimelech as well as passing on the lineage of Boaz. Obed's life is significant in that he had a son Jesse, who was the father of David who became the greatest king of Israel.

READ RUTH 1–4.

A Closer Look at the Text

There are often jokes about "the in-laws" and the issues that come with the blending of family ideas and values that arise with marriage. For Naomi and her two daughters-in-law there appears to have been a very sweet relationship. Naomi shows great kindness and concern for these two women. Knowing that she had nothing to offer them and no means to provide when she returned to her home country, she encouraged them to stay in their own land. It would be hard enough for an Israelite widow, let alone two Moabite (foreign) widows to survive in Israel. However, we see something very rare in the character of Ruth; we see a deep-rooted compassion and love for her mother-in-law that caused her to put aside her own needs in order to care for this woman.

In our day, we can miss how big a sacrifice Ruth was willing to make to stay with Naomi. She was willing to turn her back on everything that was important for a person in her day. First, she was willing to leave her homeland and everything familiar. She was willing to leave her family for Naomi. We do not know how long she had been married into this family, but the commitment was strong enough to walk away from her own biological family (even to be buried away from them in a foreign land). Along with her homeland and family she also committed to abandon her native religion. In short, she left all the things that would bring a sense of comfort and protection in exchange for staying with an aging widow with little or no hope for a decent future. Remember that this time period offered little opportunity for a woman. Ruth's best hope for a good future would be tied to her opportunity to marry well. As seen in the text, Naomi recognized this fact and realized that Ruth would have little opportunity to find this security in Israel. Wasn't this the main argument that persuaded Orpah to remain in Moab? (1:8–15)

We will see Ruth's dedication to Naomi in chapters 3 and 4. However, her commitment expressed in 1:16-17 is impressive. When Ruth pleads with Naomi not to pressure her to go back to her family, she makes the statement, "For wherever you stay, I will stay." The phrase is literally "spend the night" and may be in response to the immediate travels ahead, but also could be a reference to the fact that there was no certainty they would even have a place to stay or permanent home once they arrived in Israel. She furthers her commitment by making an oath in 1:17 that she will not even be buried in her homeland with her family; she would not leave her mother-in-law except by death. The strength of the oath is indicated by her mention that if she should leave Naomi by any other means than death, then God should put her to death in the same manner as an animal sacrificed in the oath procedure.

The story does not elaborate on the reasons for Ruth's dedication to Naomi, but from the text we can see that the older woman is in great distress. She states that "the LORD's hand has turned against me" (1:13). She tells the women of Bethlehem not to call her Naomi but rather to call her "Mara, because the Almighty has made my life very bitter" (1:20). She complains that the Lord had taken her husband and sons away from her, saying that He had afflicted her and brought misfortune on her (1:21). Not only was Naomi's family gone, but she also felt afflicted and abandoned by God. How could Ruth leave her at this point? She must have had to weigh out what it would cost her to stay with Naomi and take care of her in her distress. This is where we see the example of faithful compassion and kindness as well as a disregard for her own well-being. We see a covenant loyalty that is continually on display in God and was on display through Ruth's life.

Probably many of us at one time or another have made a commitment or sacrificed on the behalf of others, but how far have we been willing to go to fulfill our promise or commitment to others? Often there can be a willingness to help or encourage others right up to the point when it becomes costly or an inconvenience to our own lives. In chapter 2 we see true commitment on display—character that most likely makes many of us uncomfortable in comparison. Ruth's commitment went beyond words and into action by traveling to Israel. In order to provide for her mother-in-law, Ruth is described as one who worked all day in the fields, picking up the grain that the Israelites under the Law were to leave behind for the poor to glean (see 2:7, 17). She not only brought back the grain to Naomi for sale, but also "kept back" some of the lunch she had been offered by Boaz so that she could share it with her mother-in-law.

Character Revealed Through a Commitment to Selfless Interests

A quick read through the Book of Ruth reveals a multitude of topics and truths one could study. For our study, we have focused on Ruth's selfless commitment to her mother-in-law that stood in such contrast to the people of Israel during her time. We have chosen to look at this aspect of the life of

Ruth because this theme of loyal commitment (*hesed*) is a key theme in the book and the character that was clearly meant to mirror the faithful, loving-kindness of our God. The account of Ruth does not provide many details of her understanding or relationship with God, nor does the text recount the way God worked to look after Ruth apart from the blessing by the elders at the gate (4:11) or the declaration of praise to God for the child born to Ruth and Boaz (4:14). However, Ruth's assertion that she would not return to the gods of her family but would worship the God of Naomi reveals a commitment to God. The loyalty she showed is a picture of the type of character that should be evident in anyone who has made a commitment to honor and worship God.

Ruth's commitment to her mother-in-law was not a mean-spirited indictment against Orpah's choice to return home to her family and gods. Ruth's choice showed remarkable strength and resolve to express her love for Naomi. The text clearly indicated that Naomi was devastated not only by her loss of her husband and sons, but by a sense that she had either been abandoned by God or in some way was in disfavor with God. Again there are not many details offered in the text, but Ruth puts aside any concern for her own well-being and future in order to stay with the mourning woman. To abandon one's own needs in order to express love and take care of those in need surely is witnessed throughout both the Old and New Testament. This deep sense of commitment is noticed by all involved in the story of Ruth.

The Impact of Character

GOD REWARDS THOSE WHO SHOW COMPASSION FOR OTHERS OVER THEIR OWN NEEDS. Throughout the Old and New Testament there is a call for God's people to show compassion to those who are hurting or cannot take care of themselves. However, often it will cost a person to show compassion to others. In Ruth's case, she had to let go of her own needs as a young widow. She left her home and apparently her best opportunity to remarry and have security and a family. Yet, this selfless compassion did not go unnoticed by God. In fact, Ruth became the example God was looking for during a time when Israel was known for a lack of loyalty and compassion. As Ruth stepped out in kind loyalty, God stepped out and orchestrated events to give her an equally kind husband who would take care of her. God also brought her the joy of a child who would restore the honor and family line of Naomi.

GOD RECOGNIZES AND USES PEOPLE OF LOYAL CHARACTER FOR HIS PURPOSES. The last verse of the Book of Ruth is very important: "and to Obed was born Jesse, and to Jesse David " (Ruth 4:22 NASB). Ruth had no idea that her loyalty toward Naomi would bring her into the central purposes of God for Israel and ultimately all of mankind (through the line of Christ). God chooses to use her in the family line of King David. The Book of Ruth reveals that while the people of God were far from Him and in disarray, God preserved His plan and people through the life of a young Moabite widow with a selfless loyalty. When the people of God were not loyal to Him, He found a young woman of loyal character who could serve as an example of faithful sacrifice as well as provide a wonderful heritage for God's anointed king, David.

A Challenge for Our Day

The Book of Ruth does not go into detail concerning her relationship with God, but it displays a faithful self-sacrificing loyalty in this young woman who serves as a clear example for God's people, and it is certainly recognized and rewarded by God. Ruth's commitment to look out for Naomi's needs over her own serves as a challenge for each of us as followers of Christ. How quick are you to look at your own needs or carefully evaluate how much it will inconvenience or cost you to care for those in your family, church, neighborhood, or community? Do we simply show a loyalty toward others in word rather than deed? What do your actions reveal about the depth of your compassionate commitment toward those God has entrusted to you? In a world that lacks a sense of self-sacrifice, faithfulness to commitments and relationships, could God use you as an example of faithful commitment to a watching world?

Further Study

- We have only examined Ruth's character in this chapter. However, take time to go back through the Book of Ruth and notice how Boaz's integrity, honor, and commitment serve as an example of godly character. His example challenges the standards of our day as well.
- Saul's son, Jonathan, provides a valuable study of one who sacrificed much to remain loyal to his commitment to David. As Saul's son, Jonathan was in line for the throne, which God had promised to David. However, Jonathan opposed his father as well as his own birthright to faithfully honor his commitment to David (see 1 Samuel 20).

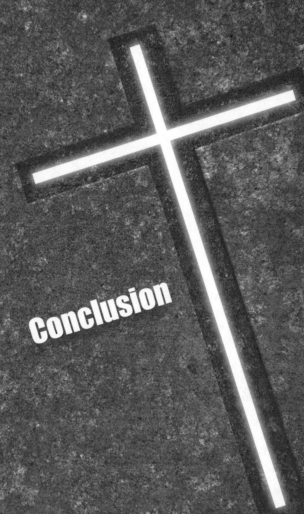

Conclusion

Character in Our Day: Why It Still Makes a Difference

CHAPTER 20

e do not have to look far to see that character is no longer a prerequisite for success in our culture. Politicians, religious and community leaders, business leaders, and individuals have demonstrated that we live in *a culture that values results above character.* We have segregated our private lives from our public ones, and our faith is a matter of personal conviction and no longer a player in the public square—unless we feel our rights have been violated; then we can sue to have our religious voice heard. Character and integrity are optional to the bottom line—unless the lack of either threatens that same bottom line by negative publicity. We depend on spin, not truth, to clear our soiled character, and we count on sound bytes and news clips to be authentic portraits of those we elect to office. Companies hide unfair and unethical practices behind carefully produced advertising campaigns and, sadly, churches sometimes cover up the unseemly messes of their leaders and their spending habits in order to portray a benevolent image to the community.

These broad observations boil and bring to the surface the need for God's people to be people of character—godly character—character as revealed in the person of Jesus Christ.

We believe having a godlike character is as distinct from our culture today as it was when God called Abraham to leave Ur or when Jesus called Peter to leave his nets. *Character, a heart filled with God's Spirit and intentions, mattered then and it is the difference-maker now.* We have not told these ancient stories as moral parables for post-modern Christians to remember or for them to long for "the good old days." We believe that these God-authored narratives hold the keys to having God-honoring character in a culture that no longer values nor supports the basic tenets and lifestyles of those who trust Jesus to be the Christ, the Son of God.

We also believe these stories hold universal and timeless realities of character that survive, no matter the circumstance or values in any global community. Character—Christlike character—matters wherever God's people have been planted and called out to be His church. Whether imprisoned in an atheistic country or free to speak your mind in a public place, character that consistently reflects the heart and love of God still makes a difference in the scheme of God's purposes and eternally impacts the lives of people.

We have tried to spell out aspects of character which you can apply to your life in each case study. We want you to become familiar with each person in the biblical stories and to wrestle with how their story is your story. How are their struggles your struggles? Can God work in your life as God did in theirs? We trust God's leading in their lives can be a window into how God can lead in your life. Along with those particular applications of character we want to draw a couple of general axioms about character that we believe will aid you in the development of your character.

Action unsupported by character ultimately nullifies the action. Don't fall into the trap of thinking that you can "fake it 'til you make it." People do not tolerate words and actions from people who say one thing but do another or who perform public acts of service and kindness, while their private lives do not match up to their message. For example, when people discovered William J. Bennett had a gambling habit that lost him millions of dollars in Las Vegas, his writings and dialogue about virtue and moral outrage lost their potency. Integrity must be the norm for Christians who live out their faith in front of others—and we all do! There is no such thing as a "private" life from a biblical worldview. Our lives are our witness. People will accept a confession of weakness and sin from a friend or leader and allow him or her time for restoration long before they accept someone who has been hiding a sinful habit until others discover that sin and make it public. No matter the power of your spin machine, if your character does not match your actions, you have lost your witness with your audience.

Jesus told His followers that they were to let their "light shine before men in such a way that they may see [their] good works, and glorify [their] Father who is in heaven" (Matthew 5:16 NASB). But good works shining before others is not enough. This is why Jesus also taught that we are not to display our acts of kindness, like giving alms or praying in public, in order to be seen. The religious people who wanted attention did that (Matthew 6:1–8). Did Jesus contradict Himself in the same message? Absolutely not. He exposed the difference between who we really are—bearing the light of the world, Jesus, in our lives—and who we want others to think we are—pious, upright people. Motive is generated in the heart, and the heart holds our true self. If you are truly "the light of the world" through your relationship with Christ, then "good works" will point to the true Light in your life. On the other hand, trying to make others think you are the light of the world by acting piously will fail when life situations expose the true makeup of your heart and character.

Another general axiom that relates to character is that the *spoken words in authentic relationship* is how God changes our hearts. We have access to more data today than at any time in history. Words come to us wirelessly at rates our ancestors could not even imagine. Images and sounds form so rapidly that 15 minutes later we cannot remember the message they tried to communicate to us. Words and images flood past us like the swollen

Mississippi River after a torrential rainfall. So, how do we who hold the life–changing message of God's love in Christ Jesus get the "word" out? How is it possible in a rapidly changing, data-saturated world to live out God's message through our words and actions?

The words we speak must come from a heart that is in authentic relationship with God. We believe that just as God spoke His Word in relationship with His people in history, in the same way God's people today are most effective when they *speak the Word of God in authentic relationship* with God and others. A characteristic of God revealed in Scripture is that God speaks. God spoke to Abraham (Genesis 12:1–3) to Moses (Exodus 3:4), and the prophets' only authority was that "the Lord spoke" to them (for example, Isaiah 8:5 and Jeremiah 14:14). "God speaks" is a foundational belief of the Christian faith.

Jesus was the spoken Word of God "in-fleshed" as a man. Of all the images God could have revealed to John the Apostle, God chose "word" as the metaphor that described His Son's coming to us. Jesus was the Word. Jesus spoke, and unclean spirits fled. Jesus spoke, and storms ceased. Jesus spoke, and people fell backwards. Jesus was the spoken Word of God in flesh.

God spoke His word in covenant relationship with people. From Abraham-who embodied the old covenant of promise—to Jesus—who is the "new covenant" of God's relationship with those who trust Him-God created a relationship with people when He spoke His Word to them. When the "Word became flesh," God exposed His heart and plans in the person of Jesus. God sent His only Son as a human being who would befriend the lost and help the faithful experience the at-hand kingdom of God. He Jesus touched the outcast and scolded the religious with words born on grace and love. But the foundation for His words was a relationship-an authentic relationship with a people and with individuals. People heard His words because He had a relationship with them. To His earthly family in Nazareth, to His friends Mary, Martha, and Lazarus in Bethany, to His disciples, and even to religious leaders in Jerusalem, Jesus spoke into their lives through relationship.

But the most important relationship Jesus had was with His Father in heaven. We get an intimate look at Jesus' relationship with the Father in the Gospel According to John. There John recorded Jesus' explanation to His students that "I am in the Father, and that the Father is in me. . . . The words I say to you I do not speak on my own authority. Rather, it is the Father, living in me, who is doing his work" (John 14:10). Jesus also revealed how His life revolved around the Father's leadership in His life when he declared, "For I have come down from heaven not to do my will but to do the will of him who sent me" (John 6:38). Jesus' earthly relationships were formed out of His relationship with His Father. This real, yet mysterious, relationship formed Jesus' character and was the basis into which He spoke His lifesaving words.

For those who trust Jesus today, we must first have an intimate, vital relationship with God in order to have the kinds of authentic relationships into which we can speak the life-changing message of God. Just as Jesus had a relationship with His Father, we must have a relationship with the Triune God in order to have trust-filled relationships with others. To be an effective follower of Jesus, to speak the message of God's redeeming love into the lives of others, we must know Jesus, and this knowledge comes only through a relationship with Jesus.

God's Word spoken in authentic relationship is how God continues to spread the message of salvation to all peoples. ***This is why character still matters.*** *Word and relationship are built upon the foundation of character,* and neither is valid unless built upon the Rock of a relationship with God through His Son, Jesus.

CHAPTER 21

Preparing for God to Mold Your Character

f character is the foundation for our life, witness, and effectiveness as followers of Jesus, how do we prepare ourselves for God to mold our character? While God is the One who develops our character, we are responsible to place ourselves in the position for Him to do so. What can we do to prepare ourselves for God to mold our character?

The answer is found in spending time with God in His Word, in His creation, in the needs of others, and in fellowship with fellow followers. These are not new practices we share with you. They are ancient, time-honored pathways that help you make room in your heart for God to mold your character. You can't develop godly character for yourself. Only the Holy Spirit living in your heart can do that. You can, however, provide the space for the Spirit to do His sanctifying work in your life in order to produce the "fruit" of His presence (Galatians 5:22). Let's look at some ways you can prepare for God to mold your character.

Spend time with God in His Word. The Bible is the written Word of God, which reveals God's heart and purposes. You cannot have the character of God without knowing God through time spent reading the Bible, entering the story, and finding your place in it. Scripture memorization is important, but familiarity through consistent reading and meditation on the Word may be more helpful in seizing the story of the Bible. To possess character that makes a difference, you must know what godly character looks like from God's revealed Word. The case studies in this book are examples from which you can know God and how He desires to mold your character.

Spend time in God's creation. We have built environments that keep us from the good creation of God. Urban and suburban structures wall us away from the beauty and power of God in His created order. We believe part of the "fullness of time" into which Jesus came was a world in which people knew the rhythms of the seasons and the cycles of growing things. Jesus' parables came from agriculture and some of His most powerful signs were performed in nature, not to mention in the lives of people! Spend time in God's creation, even if it is in a city park. Listen to the birds, feel the wind, see the beauty of flowers and trees. Observe God's most precious creation, people. Recall Jesus' parables and teaching that came from His created order. Read some of the psalms thanking God for revealing His character in creation and praise Him for beauty and the breath He has given you for His purposes.

Spend time in the needs of others. To have the character of Christ is to have a love for those who are outcast, hurting, hungry, and ill-served by others. Christlike character displays a sacrificial love that enters the suffering of others. Jesus said He did not come to be served but to serve and to give His life as a ransom for many (Mark 10:45). If we follow Jesus, we will follow Him to the leper, widow, prisoner, and into the grief of those around us in order to serve them. One way to prepare yourself for God to mold your character is to leave the comfort of the life you have built for yourself and enter the pain and suffering of another. This might be in the life of a loved one who is suffering with cancer, or it also might be traveling to a culture you do not know in order to serve in the name of Jesus among a people in which you are the minority. God calls us to serve others in His name. Service to others who cannot pay us back or who may not praise us for our actions is a crucible that forms Christ's character within us.

Spend time with fellow followers. Jesus lived and ministered in a fellowship of friends. Men and women traveled with him as He demonstrated and proclaimed the at-hand kingdom of God. He shared His grief, joys, prayers, and plans with these servants-turned-friends (John 15:15). He molded their character by spending time with them day and night. When the Holy Spirit formed the church during the festival of Pentecost, *fellowship with fellow followers of Jesus was a hallmark of the movement.* They worshipped together, were in each other's homes, and served those in need by sharing what they had in common with everyone (Acts 2:42–47). Would it not follow that you and I need fellowship with other followers of Jesus in order for God to mold our character? The New Testament is filled with instructions for us to meet together, to bear one another's burdens, to pray together, and to serve together in Jesus' name.

Our families (Norman's and Gene's) belong to a local fellowship of followers. These local expressions of the body of Christ provide ways in which God forms our character and with whom we can live out God's call on our lives. Within the larger body of the local church we belong to small groups with whom we share life. These are people who know us well enough to call us out if our words and actions don't match our true character, which they observe on a regular basis.

God will mold your character into the likeness of Christ if you will submit to His leadership in your life. Make room in your life for the Holy Spirit to change you as you spend time with His Word, in His creation, serving others, and with fellow followers of Jesus.

CHAPTER 22

Allowing God to Make a Difference Through You

T

he development of our character is never simply for our own lives. God's work in our lives is for the purpose of working *through* our lives to impact His world. Character does not only matter simply so that you will be a better person and contribute to society. The stakes are much higher than that. Your life has value beyond what you provide for your family or the company's bottom line or your service to your community. **YOUR LIFE HAS AN ETERNAL IMPACT!**

God desires to make an eternal difference in the lives of others through you. This has been true from the beginning of the Story. The Bible tells us that God chose Abraham and his descendants so he would be "a blessing" (Genesis 12:2). God did not choose Abraham to bless him for his family's sake or so he would be the richest man in the world. He blessed him so the world would know the God of Abraham, Isaac, and Jacob was the One True God. Jesus, too, chose His disciples so they would be His "witnesses" to the ends of the earth (Acts 1:8). He did not reveal He was the Messiah so they could tell their friends they met Him first. Jesus revealed Himself to them, spent time with them, died and was raised from the dead for them so the world would know the love of God revealed in His Son, Jesus. The Holy Spirit formed the church not so its members would be well off and happy in a broken and hurting world. God created the church as a mission outpost for the kingdom of God in which the "called out ones" in Christ gather and scatter to impact the world for Christ until He returns.

A mystery of whom God chose to serve Him is that God did not choose those who would be our obvious choices. God chose people for what He saw in their hearts—hearts that were not necessarily pure, but they were moldable. God told Samuel when it was time to choose the second king of Israel not to look on outward appearance as people did to judge a person because God looked on the heart (1 Samuel 16:7). *Character is a matter of the heart,* and this is where God looks for those He chooses to serve Him. From the biblical case studies in this book you have seen God often chose the weak, the youngest, or—in every case—anyone but the *perfect!* God chose those whose hearts were moldable and soft to His leading. They did not have the character of God when God chose them, but in most cases they were more like God at the end of their stories than when God first chose them—when He entered the picture.

God chooses the humble. The proud do not need God's help, or so they think. Humble people empowered by God's Spirit and guided by His Word are the game-changers in kingdom life. Only character molded and empowered by God can make an eternal difference in others. This includes you. If you will humble yourself before God, confess your sin and weakness, trust Jesus to be who He said He was and submit to His leadership in your life, God can mold your character and empower you like the people in these case studies—and like He has done in millions of others since them—to make an eternal difference where you live.

The case studies in this book are examples of God-molded character and the differences these people made in the lives of others for the glory of God. *Your life is a case study.* People observe you, draw conclusions about you, and they make judgments about the God you confess based on what you do and say. If we were to write your case study through the eyes of God, what would we see you do? What would we hear you say? Would your character be anything like what you describe to others? We are not perfect ourselves, so we must ask these questions along with you.

Our prayer is that God will use these case studies of real people, who were chosen and guided by the one true God, to mold your character so it too will make an eternal difference.

Your life can make a difference. Your character will be the difference between a life molded and used by God and a life molded and lived by you. Our prayer is that you will allow God to mold your character so He can make an eternal difference with your life for His glory.

Norman Blackaby
Gene Wilkes
Reformation Day

Leadership Resources

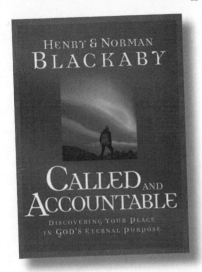

Called and Accountable
*Discovering Your Place in
God's Eternal Purpose*
Henry T. Blackaby and
Norman C. Blackaby
ISBN-13: 978-1-59669-047-9
N064153 • $19.99

TeamsWork
*A No-Nonsense Approach for
Achieving More Together*
Joyce A. Mitchell
ISBN-13: 978-1-59669-211-4
N084136 • $12.99

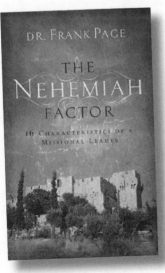

The Nehemiah Factor
*16 Characteristics of a
Missional Leader*
Dr. Frank S. Page
ISBN-13: 978-1-59669-223-7
N084146 • $14.99

Available in bookstores everywhere.
For information about these books
or any New Hope product,
visit newhopedigital.com.

New Hope® Publishers is a division of WMU®, an international organization that challenges Christian believers to understand and be radically involved in God's mission.

For more information about WMU, go to: wmu.com.

More information about New Hope books can be found at newhopedigital.com.

New Hope books may be purchased at your local bookstore.

Use the QR reader on your
smartphone to visit us online at
newhopedigital.com

If you've been blessed by this book, we would like to hear your story.
The publisher and author welcome your comments and
suggestions at: newhopereader@wmu.org.